Skeletons In The Closet

by Therese Fisher, A.G.

HERITAGE BOOKS, INC.

Maps on pages viii and 72
by Nick Ackermann

Other Heritage Books by the author:
Marriages in Virginia:
Spotsylvania County, 1851-1900 and Orange County, 1851-1867

Marriages in the New River Valley, Virginia:
Montgomery, Floyd, Pulaski and Giles Counties

Marriage Records of the City of Fredericksburg and the County of Stafford,
Virginia, 1851-1900

Vital Records of Three Burned Counties:
Births, Marriages and Deaths of King and Queen, King William,
and New Kent Counties, Virginia, 1680-1860

Marriages of Caroline County, Virginia, 1777-1853

Marriage Records of the City of Fredericksburg, and of Orange, Spotsylvania,
and Stafford Counties, Virginia, 1722-1850

Published 2001 by
HERITAGE BOOKS, INC.
1540E Pointer Ridge Place, Bowie, Maryland 20716
1-800-398-7709 — www.heritagebooks.com

ISBN 0-7884-1886-6

CONTENTS

LIST OF ILLUSTRATIONS

TWO VIEWS OF THE RAPPAHANNOCK RIVER

Preface

MURDER. Not a pretty word. The act referred to is even less attractive. Why, then, write a book on murders?

What started out as a genealogical study, evolved into a much more complex work with historical and sociological tendencies.

Beginning with the genealogical aspect of the book, I combed court and newspaper records in a search for murder victims or perpetrators. Curiously, few of the victims or murderers appeared in any other records normally equated with genealogical research. Some of the reasons for this are dealt with from the sociological aspect, others from the historical aspect. This is not surprising to genealogists, since the study of genealogy, when done in depth, requires a study of the social and historic details for the area.

The area I selected was one in which I had easy access to all types of records. The Rappahannock River was the thread that tied all the areas together, from its headwaters in Madison County down to the "falls of the Rappahannock" near Fredericksburg. In some cases, the river itself played a part, such as in the numerous suicides and accidental drownings that occurred. In other cases, it was the avenue of escape for a murderer. In the cases of baby John or Jane Doe, the river was the murder weapon.

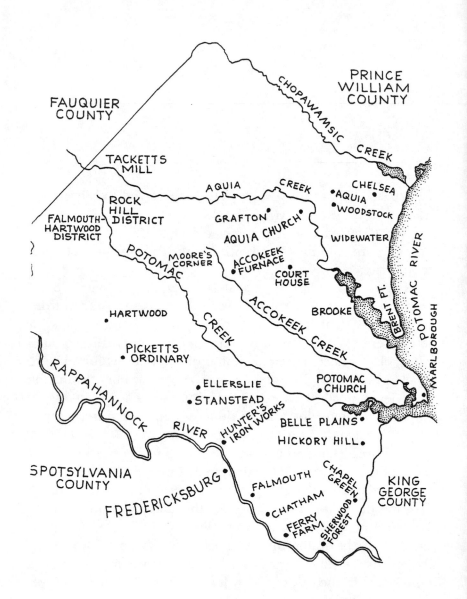

The records I selected were much more arbitrarily chosen than the site or the time period. While I had, on the average, one murder per year for the 200-year time span that I chose, not every murder's details are included in this book. I began by selecting murders that seemed unusual in some way. The number was then further decreased by the availability of enough details related to the murderer or the victim or the act itself to produce more than a name and date. I finally divided the book into categories and selected a number of murders for each category.

For the sake of historical research, I included a list of all the names of either murderer or victim (or both, when available) and the year that the murder occurred in a separate appendix. Throughout the book I retained the spelling of the names as found in the records. There was no attempt to standardize the name spellings.

Another appendix that I included lists the numbers of murders that occurred in several of the political jurisdictions covered by the scope of this book. Not all are included, mainly because figures are not available for all jurisdictions for all time periods. Another appendix gives the census figures for each of the jurisdictions for the time period of the book. For the time periods previous to the first federal census in 1790, I used tithables for the county, or tax records, or I calculated the population using average household size and available names and numbers. The figures for census years are from the federal census. A comparison of the population figures and the number of murders that occurred in that area proved interesting but not conclusive. Obviously, more variables were at work than mere numbers.

One of the overall observations that I made was that there seemed to be a rise in murders a couple of years after a war ended. A psychologist or sociologist may be able to add twenty-first-century figures to that, to either confirm or disprove my observation.

From the historical standpoint, this book evolved as a product of the time periods included. The earliest court records for this area, 1722, helped determine the beginning point of my research, although there were tales of a murder that occurred in Stafford in the late 1600's involving an Indian and some of the settlers of the Stafford frontier. If local legend and claims can be considered true, the tribe may have been the same as Pocahontas's tribe. But I did not want to deal in legend and hearsay. So I began with the earliest court records. The ending point was the real challenge. So many interesting murders occurred in the twentieth century that I had a hard time drawing a line. But concern for the privacy of some of the families of victims or murderers who were still alive and in the area led me to end the book at a time period that was highly improbable of having any living participants.

Acknowledgments

I **RECEIVED** a great deal of help via the computerization of the Fredericksburg District Court records, which was due to the efforts of Barry McGhee. Ann Amadori, while processing papers for the computer data bank, alerted me to several murders that had been buried in unindexed court records. Paula Felder opened her vast store of notes and research on Spotsylvania County and Fredericksburg to me, which greatly increased my resources. Rebecca Light provided me with several leads and tales of murder that she discovered while researching Civil War era records. Barbara Kirby guided me through Stafford County's files. Bob Hodge allowed me to use his history of Alum Spring. His indexes for the local newspapers were invaluable aids in finding cases both covered by court records and those that, for whatever reason, were not included in the district court records. Noel Harrison, through his natural inquisitiveness and incredible knowledge of the Civil War, helped put me on to a murder that I would have passed over as inconclusive, but that turned out to be one of the most interesting murders I studied. I publicly acknowledge my indebtedness to all of these historians and offer many thanks to them for their assistance.

Definitions

...that which makes history the richest of philosophies and the most genial pursuit of humanity is the spirit that is breathed into it by the thoughts and feelings of former generations, interpreted in actions and incidents that disclose the passions, motives, and ambition of men and open us a view of the actual life of our forefathers. When we can contemplate the people of a past age employed in their own occupations, observe their habits and manners, comprehend their policy and their methods of pursuing it, our imagination is quick to clothe them with the flesh and blood of human brotherhood and to bring them into full sympathy with our individual nature. History then becomes a world of living figures—a theatre that presents to us a majestic drama, varied by alternate scenes of the grandest achievements and the most touching episodes of human existence.

John Pendleton Kennedy
1857

IN THE judge's instructions to the jury in the 1893 case of the *Commonwealth v. Jackson*, the criteria for manslaughter and murder were described. These would be helpful in understanding how juries determined how to charge the defendant.

"If the jury believe beyond a reasonable doubt that the prisoner killed the accused in a sudden fight without justification and without previous intent to kill, she is guilty of voluntary manslaughter the punishment of which is from one to five years in the penitentiary.

"If the jury believe beyond a reasonable doubt that the prisoner maliciously and unjustifiably inflicted a wound on the deceased with the intent to kill her from which wound the deceased died, then the prisoner is guilty of murder.

"Which may be either murder in the 1st degree or the second degree. If it was a willful deliberate and premeditated killing it was murder in the first degree. Otherwise murder in the second."

As a matter of comparison, the instructions to the jury in the case of the *Commonwealth v. Kendall*, 1924 were as follows:

"Murder is the unlawful killing of any person with malice aforethought.

"The court instructs the jury that murder is distinguished as murder in the first degree and as murder in the second degree,

"Every homicide is presumed to be murder in the second degree. In order to raise the offense to murder in the first degree, the burden of proof is upon the Commonwealth and to reduce the offense to manslaughter, the burden of proof is upon the prisoner.

"The court instructs the jury, that on a charge of murder, malice is presumed from the fact of the killing; and when the killing is proven, unattended with circumstances of palliation, the burden of disproving malice is thrown upon the accused.

"The court further tells the jury that whenever the killing is willful, deliberate and premeditated the law infers malice from this fact.

"The court further instructs the jury that the rule of law is that a man shall be taken to intend that which he does, or which is the necessary consequence of his act.

"The court instructs the jury that in order to constitute murder in the first degree, it is not necessary that the intent to kill should have existed for any particular length of time. It may be formed at the very moment of the killing, or at any time previously.

[some repetitive instructions omitted]

"The court instructs the jury that if you believe from the evidence beyond a reasonable doubt that previous to the time of the killing of the deceased, there existed a grudge on the part of the accused towards the deceased, and that the accused had previously declared his purpose to kill the deceased, and that the accused had previously declared his intent to kill the deceased, and that the accused killed the deceased in execution of such previously existing grudge, and pursuant to such previously declared purpose, then he is guilty of murder in the first degree."

There were four more pages of instructions, but the main ideas presented in those four pages are contained in these included instructions.

Dr. David Lester, in his book, *Questions And Answers About Murder,* defines homicide as an unintentional killing. When negligence by the killer results in the death of a victim it is called involuntary manslaughter.

"Murder is the unlawful killing of a person."[1]

"The Unwritten law is all portion of the law, observed and administered in the courts, which has not been enacted or promulgated in the form of a statute or ordinance, including the unenacted portions of the common law, general and particular customs having the force of law, and the rules, principles and maxims established by judicial precedents or the successive like decisions of the courts."[2]

---

[1] David Lester, *Questions And Answers About Murder.* (Philadelphia: The Charles Press, 1991)

[2] Black's Law Dictionary, Seventh Edition

 **Uxorcide**

HAISLIP (1859)

PERUSING my notes of the 200 years of murders occurring along the Rappahannock River, I have found many tragic, some strange—but none were common or dull. Unexpectedly, I noticed that there were very few murders that were inflicted on one spouse by the other spouse. As a matter of fact, the case that follows was almost unique in several aspects. It involved the Haislip family of Spotsylvania and later, Fredericksburg.

James D. Haslop (also spelled Haslip, Heislip, Heislop, Hazlop) was the son of James & Lucy Haislip of Spotsylvania.[1] The 1850 Census of Culpeper County listed his occupation as a stonemason and bricklayer.[2] His services were much in demand in the surrounding communities that were in the proc-

---

[1] Death records for Fredericksburg, indexed by Robert Hodge
[2] 1850 Federal Census, Culpeper County, p. 271

ess of replacing older wooden structures with new buildings of brick and mortar.

With a steady job, James was ready to find a wife and start his family. He found his wife among his cousins. Eliza Kinesn Heislop was the daughter of Horace Heislop and Sally Ann Hart.[3] Horace was related to James's father, James. Additionally, both Horace's and James's wives were Harts, so it seems very possible that James and Eliza were cousins twice.

James and Eliza were married in about 1842, probably in Spotsylvania. No record of their marriage exists in the area. The marriage date is an estimate based on the age of their eldest known child. He was about 23 and she about 20 years old at the time of their marriage. Soon after their marriage, the young couple moved to Culpeper, where James worked as a stonemason. While there, at least two of their daughters were born, Lovely V. and Lucy O. or C.

The lure of the larger town of Fredericksburg, with all the new building that was taking place, and the presence of both of their families nearby had them pulling up roots from Culpeper and moving into the city of Fredericksburg by 1859.

Alcohol was available to the citizenry of the area until Prohibition in the twentieth century. Taverns and ordinaries dispensed roughly produced drinks as well as wines and brandies. Abuse of alcohol was as prevalent in the mid-nineteenth century as it is today, with the same unfortunate side affects of abusive behavior, carelessness and (as it was phrased then) debauchery. When James began drinking cannot be determined for certain, but it is apparent that by November of 1859, his alcoholic habits were such that his neighbors were aware of his drinking binges. He had been taken to court on a couple of occasions for assaulting various townspeople. It also appears that he had begun to abuse his wife.

Sometime on Friday, November 6, 1859, James began to snack on a bowl of chestnuts. He may also have been drinking that afternoon. By evening, he had begun to have violent

---

[3] Marriage License in Fredericksburg, VA

spasms, his body going rigid for a time, and then relaxing. He would gasp for breath while his body was in one of those convulsions. He occasionally yelled out incoherently but then returned to a normal manner of speaking. The visitors that had been in the Heislip home that night began to show signs of concern and discomfort at James's condition. The men had decided that James was violently drunk and determined that he was so drunk he would in some way offend the ladies that were present. To spare them, one of the male visitors, Mr. Smith, suggested the ladies leave the room. Mr. Smith followed and as, Benjamin F. Curl was getting ready to leave, James asked him to stay.

"Don't leave me," he implored. "I have something to say to you before I die."

Benjamin remained with him, perplexed and shocked by James's premonition. But the worst was yet to come.

"I have a load on my stomach. They have given me a dose." Benjamin was too shocked to even ask who "they" were. "If I die, I wish you to have me cut open and examined. It will show itself."[4]

Soon after that, James was dead.

By eleven o'clock the next morning, Bery Clarke, a justice of the peace, was asked to stand in as coroner. He called upon James A. Taylor to summon a coroner's jury to examine James Heslop and determine the cause of death. J. W. Levin, W. J. Chesly, John L. Kinight, H. G. Doggett, Moris Montgomery, George Gravitt, J. Stone, Mr. H. Smith, Nim. Burke, Peleg Clarke, John Rogers and Charles Williams were summoned to view the body. After withdrawing to the home of Mr. Bowman, a neighbor of the Heislops, they determined that based on the physical evidence, James came to his death from "cold, concerning a general stimulation of the system subsequent to and

[4] Deposition of Benjamin Curl, Coronor's Inquest, Fredericksburg District Court

consequent upon exposure after debauch."[5]   In other words, he died of exposure after a night of drinking.

A couple of weeks later, James Skinner and his son were visiting Eliza Heislop. While there, the little boy found the bowl of chestnuts and reached in to take a few. Eliza stopped him and brought the bowl over to his father. Mixed in with the chestnuts were one and a half "dog buttons." Eliza stated that if the child had taken them, it would have killed him.

"Dog buttons, dogs nut, Quaker buttons, ratsbane and poison nut" are all common names for *strychnos nux vomica*. Its poisonous properties were well known in the 19th and early 20th centuries. Many farm households kept a supply of this on hand to poison rats, prairie dogs, wild dogs, feral cats and other pests on farms. While all parts of the tree are poisonous, it is the five seeds shaped like flattened disks (chestnut shaped) inside each fruit that are the most poisonous. When given in poisonous amounts, it causes violent convulsions, rictus, spasms, rapid heartbeat, and would be a most horrible death.[6]   The tablets were available from physicians and pharmacists at this time in Fredericksburg. Eliza stated to Skinner that she bought them from Dr. Cook to kill their dog.[7]

The dying statement of James Heislip to Benjamin Curl helped fuel rumors that began to circulate about the cause of Heislip's death. Bery Clark summoned Frank and Duck Hazelop,[8] Curl, Skinner, Wade Hix, Mr. Chin, J. M. Edrington and Bluert Hayslop[9] to the mayor's office at eight o'clock that night in an attempt to determine whether Heislop was

---

[5] Ibid.

[6] *King's American Dispensatory,* Harvey Wickes Felter, M.D. and John Uri Lloyd, Phr. M., Ph. D., 1898.

[7] Deposition of James Skinner, Coroner's Inquest, Fredericksburg District Court

[8] The marriage record for Frank Heslup and Placid B. Heslup in 1858 states that Frank was the son of James and Lucy Heslup, and Placid B. was the daughter of William and Harriet Heslup.

[9] This may be Rice Heslop, son of James and Lucy Heslop.

murdered or whether he died from exposure, as the coroner's jury determined.

Apparently, Bery decided that there was not sufficient evidence to justify the charge of murder in the case of James Heislop. The death of James Heislop was never brought to court.

In 1866 Eliza Heislop married Horace Gatchell, a saddler from Maine. There is no further record of her or her daughters in Fredericksburg.

SOCIOLOGISTS have studied and debated whether or not the presence of a weapon incites people to commit murder. One of the conclusions they have reached is that armed robberies are more likely to result in a murder if the robber has a gun, rather than any other weapon. Whether this is cause or effect is hotly debated. Common sense seems to dictate that the presence of a weapon during a quarrel would be more likely to result in a murder. However, real life situations, as opposed to the artificial laboratory environment used by sociologists, suggest that a weapon is not the critical factor in whether an argument escalates into murder or not, as the following case illustrates.

BRANSON (1800)

MADISON COUNTY, Virginia, was formed in 1793 from the southwestern part of Culpeper County. It is a very rural county with a stable population. Its population in 1800 was 8,322, comparable to that of Stafford County.

Vinson, or, Vincent Branson was tried for the murder of his wife, Lydia, on February 25, 1800, in Madison County, Virginia. The case was tried in the District Court of Fredericksburg, which had jurisdiction over Madison County, and the notes are as follows. (All repetitive legal language has been deleted; other than that, the transcript is accurate.)

INDICTMENT OF VINCENT BRANSON FOR MURDER...
WE THE GRAND JURY FIND THIS A TRUE BILL.
signed by John Lewis, Foreman

Justices present for the examination of Vinson Branson; Henry Hill, Merry Walker, Thomas Barbour, John Field, Robert Thomas, Paschal Early & Joshua Leatherer.

"The Prisoner being led to the bar, and it being demanded of him whether he was guilty of the murder aforesaid or not. He said he was not guilty. Whereupon sundry witnesses were sworn and examined and the prisoner heard in his defense. On consideration whereof it is considered by the court that for the murder aforesaid he ought to be tried before the next District Court to be holden at Fredericksburg and thereupon he is remanded to gaol. Clary Rambottom, William Hurt, John Smith, Jeremiah Jinkins, Abraham Alger, Elizabeth Cole, James Yager & Peter Fox of this County came into Court and acknowledged themselves severally indebted to his Excellency James Monroe Esq. Governor of this Commonwealth for the time being and his successors in the sum of five hundred dollars each, to be levied of their respective goods and chattels lands and tenements and to the Commonwealth rendered."
[This last statement is a bond that the witnesses made to promise that they would appear in District Court for the case of Vinson Branson. The remainder of the document is repetitive language binding the witnesses to appear in court and restating the charges.]

DISTRICT COURT OF FREDERICKSBURG,
MADISON COUNTY COURT

The jurors of the Commonwealth of and for the body of the District composed of the counties of Spotsylvania, Caroline, King George, Stafford, Orange, Culpeper and Madison, do upon their oath present that Vincent Branson, late of the county of Madison aforesaid labourer not having the fear of God before him but being moved and seduced by the instigation of the Devil, on the twenty fourth day of February in the year of our Lord one thousand and eight hundred and in the twenty fourth year of the Commonwealth with force and arms at the county of Madison aforesaid...and upon Lydia Branson...feloniously and willfully and of malice aforethought did make an assault and that the said Vincent Branson with both his hands and feet...did throw and cast...upon the ground the said Lydia Branson...then at the county last mentioned feloniously willfully and of malice aforethought did strike, beat and kick giving to the said Lydia Branson...in and upon the head, stomach, back, sides and neck of her [body]...mortal bruises. The said Lydia Branson from the said twenty fourth of February with a year aforesaid until the twenty fifth day of the same month of February in the year aforesaid...did languish and languishing...of the several mortal bruises aforesaid died....

Sworn in court April 29, 1800

"We the jury find him guilty of murder in the second degree. Eighteen years confinement.

signed by Joseph James"

"Oath do say that the said Vincent Branson is guilty of the murder aforesaid as in the Indictment against him is alleged   that the said murder is of the second degree, and that the said V.B. ought to be confined in the gaol & penitentiary for the term of ___ years. Therefore it is ordered that the sheriff of Madison County do within safely remove and convey the said A.B. [meaning V.B.] from the gaol of this district to the gaol and penitentiary house in the city of Richmond there to undergo an imprisonment at hard labour and solitary confinement for the term of ____ years (from this date) the period by the jury in their verdict prescribed and thereupon he is remanded to gaol."[10]

PUZEY (1845)

GERARD Pusey/Puzey came to Spotsylvania County some time before 1840. He seems to have been related in some fashion to Sarah or Sally Pusey. Ann Pusey may be the same person as either Sarah Pusey or Gerrard's wife, Mildred who was called Malvina in a land record.

In Spotsylvania Court of January 1844, Gerard and Ann were summoned to show cause why a road should not be changed and re-routed to run through their property. In March of that same year, Sally Pusey sold a parcel of land to Thomas Lewis. In August, she sold additional land to Richard Sorrell. In November 1845, Gerard Pusey and "Malvina," his wife, and Sarah Pusey sold land to Sanford Chancellor. Whether any of these land sales had something to do with the road that was supposed to run through their property is not immediately indicated.

---

[10] Fredericksburg District Court papers ID#560-88

In the Virginia Circuit Superior Court of Law and Chancery for Spotsylvania County, a case was brought against Mildred Puzey, late of Spotsylvania County. The charges were that on Christmas Day (December 25) 1845, "not having the fear of God before her eyes but being moved and seduced by the instigation of the Devil…[did] on Gerard Puzey, in the peace of God and of the Commonwealth, there and there being feloniously, willfully and of her malice aforethought did make an assault and that the said Mildred Puzey with a certain iron pin, which the said Mildred Puzey in her right hand, then and there had and held, the said Gerard Puzey in and upon the top of his head, and in an upon the right and left side of the forehead and in and upon the front of the forehead of him the said Gerard Puzey…did strike and beat, giving to the said Gerard Puzey by striking and beating…several mortal strokes and bruises…He the said Gerard Puzey on the twenty fifth day of December eighteen hundred and forty five…did languish and languishing did…die."

The list of witnesses for this case is interesting because of the previous land transactions. Witnesses were Sanford Chancellor, Washington Lewis, Thomas Lewis, Charles A. Harrow, Henry Jett and Hugh McGee.

Mildred was tried in May 1846. She pled not guilty and was acquitted.[11]

---

[11] Fredericksburg Court papers, ID#462-34

💀 Infanticide

EVERY parent has, at one time or another in their child's life, had the urge to become violent with their child. Sometimes a parent will even yell "I'm going to kill you if you ever do that again!" generally with only temporary intent. Occasionally, though, a parent will follow through on that spoken or unspoken threat. When that occurs, it is called infanticide, one of the most unnatural acts of violence (if any type of violence could be called natural).

No geographic area is immune to this type of murder. The largest number of murders committed on children were, by far, on infants under one year old. Usually they were newborn and abandoned to the elements or drowned in the Rappahannock River. Most were listed as John or Jane Doe, parent or name unknown.

I have included tales of children murdered by a parent from several of the areas encompassed by this book.

STEVENS (1803)

The story of Lucy Stevens is narrated in a somewhat fictional fashion. It should be noted, however, that the place description, the murder and method of the murder, the persons named and some of the dialog are taken from the court records of Spotsylvania County. The activities surrounding the actual murder are either described in the court record or surmised from the lifestyle of the time.

LUCY STEVENS wrapped a shawl around her shoulders to ward off the February chill and walked from her father's house through the golden colored field that bordered her home. The brown stalks of last year's corn rustled under her feet. A grackle called its warning to the birds pecking in the field.

The low border of honeysuckle vines that formed the boundary between her father's field and the property of Colonel Minor presented some problems for Lucy to get through. Her skirts caught in the vines that wrapped around her feet and ankles, holding her back.

She had walked about a mile. The pains that started in her back spread to her abdomen and became stronger and more frequent. Finally she sighted Colonel Minor's barn. Although the barn had been unused for a number of years, it was still in fairly good condition. Straw still covered the floor and the roof and walls were intact. Entering the barn, she sank into the straw and lay there, her body racked with the pains of childbirth.

When the time for her delivery finally came, she hoisted herself to a squatting position and lifted her skirts above the straw so as not to leave any evidence of her experience on her clothing.

At last the baby girl was pushed from her body. She lay on the straw covered in a waxy coating. Blood clung to the infant and stained the straw. The tiny arms waved in an effort to breathe. Lucy looked down at her child. As the afterbirth was expelled Lucy took the knife that was to cut the umbilical cord and severed the baby's head from her body and then cut the baby into pieces.

The evening of the same day, February 28, 1803, Daniel Tiller saw Lucy Stevens on her way home. She was coming from the direction of Colonel Minor's barn.[1]

Achilles Mills was at John Stevens' house, visiting when John's daughter, Lucy, came home. Near the house she complained of being very weak and asked for assistance in getting into the house.[2]

Wednesday afternoon Daniel Tiller was out walking with his grandson. He observed Nathaniel Stevens, brother to John Stevens, looking for something around Colonel Minor's barn. When he asked what Nathaniel was looking for he replied that he "was hunting for that he doubted he should not find." Tiller, glancing into the barn and noticing the blood in the straw, sent his little grandson home, telling him that he would be home shortly. Once the boy was gone, Tiller searched the barn with Stevens for a while. He probably guessed, or was told by Nathaniel, what they were looking for. Not finding anything and noticing that the time was getting late, he left Stevens and went home.[3]

That evening, Nathaniel Stevens and a Mr. Tombs searched the branch of the river near the barn. Tiller, returning to help with the search, found the two men standing together at the edge of the water. When they beckoned to him, he came over to discover the body of the infant cut into eight pieces. The body was brought to the home of John Stevens, who buried it.

---

[1] Deposition of Daniel Tiller Fredericksburg District Court for Spotsylvania County, ID#564-112

[2] Deposition of Achilles Mills, ID#564-112

[3] Deposition of Daniel Tiller

The next day, Thursday, March 3, Thomas Minor, a judge for the Spotsylvania Court, ordered Lucy Stevens to be apprehended and kept in the jail until her trial for the murder of her child.

On March 9, 1803, she was sent to the Spotsylvania jail. Witnesses were sworn in court on Friday, April 29, 1803, two months and one day after the murder. The brief trial held the same day in Fredericksburg District Court found Lucy Stevens not guilty of murder. The names of the jurors who could not convict a young girl for killing her newborn illegitimate baby were John Mitchum, James Bullock, Henry Thornton, Thomas McKenny, John Gale, James Vullos, William Jackson, Robert Cammack, William Beasley, Benjamin Alsop, Henry Wyat and Peter Dudly.[4]

Lucy returned to her father's home and remained there through 1810.

John Stevens' will, dated August 14, 1827, does not mention Lucy or either of her sisters. Her brother, Edward, is the only legatee and executor of his father's estate in Spotsylvania County.[5]

We are left to guess about Lucy's life after that trial in 1803. Did she marry? Did she die soon after the trial? Did her father disown her because of her terrible actions after the birth of her illegitimate daughter? Spotsylvania records are silent.

---

[4] Court papers in Fredericksburg District Court, ID#564-112
[5] Spotsylvania Will Book

GRYMES (1835)

ELIZA Grymes was a free mulatto who resided in Spotsylvania County in 1835. She seems to have lived in the vicinity of William Bernard and Colonel Gulidmus Smith.

For some reason known only to her, on August 14, 1835, she picked up a stone and beat her two-year-old son, George, to death. The child was beaten on the upper part and the back of his head and seems to have died instantly.

The Spotsylvania County sheriff took her into custody the same day, a warrant having been sworn out against her. On August 19, Peggy Smith and Harriet Grymes, a "free woman of color," were sworn as witnesses against Eliza Grymes. George Hamilton, the justice of the peace at that time, also called Lucinda (who was called "Colonel Gulidmus Smith's woman"), and Mary, a Negro woman, as witnesses.

Court was held on September 2, 1835. They believed in swift justice in those days.

In the Circuit Superior Court of Law and Chancery for Spotsylvania County, Eliza Grymes was convicted of murder in the second degree and sentenced to the penitentiary for five years. Generally the term of imprisonment for second-degree murder was twelve years. Whatever was said during the trial that caused the justices to give her the smallest possible jail term is not recorded among the court minutes.

There is no further record of Eliza Grymes.

LUCAS (1872)

A **LARGE** number of murders that occurred over the two-hundred-year period covered in this book were acts of violence. The following death was, from the indictment, listed as involuntary manslaughter. However, the circumstances surrounding this death were such that it needed to be included as one of the infanticides.

Sylvia Lucas lived in the city of Fredericksburg in 1872. She was probably among the poorer residents of that corporation. No marriage record exists for her in Fredericksburg, nor is she among the landowners of that city. It is possible that she was a person of color, since a large percentage of the Lucas residents of the city were black.

Sylvia had a daughter named Elizabeth, who lived with her. Apparently, from the indictment records, Elizabeth, then age 14, became ill around June 20, 1872. From that date until July 20, Elizabeth was given nothing to eat. As a result of her starvation and possibly her illness, she died on July 20, 1872.

Her mother, Sylvia, was charged with involuntary manslaughter by neglect and starvation. The constable and keeper of the jail in Fredericksburg, John S. G. Timberlake, was charged with the apprehension of Sylvia Lucas. The courts determined that there was sufficient evidence to try her on the involuntary manslaughter charges and set her bail at $300.00. She was unable to pay the bail amount and was thus, on July 22, remanded to jail to await her trial.

Witnesses at her trial included Dr. L. B. Rose, Milly Hall, Jerry Griny, Martha Jackson, Margaret Lewis and Annie Crutchfield.

Her jury, which included W. Aldridge, William P. Alsop, Robert W. Adams, J. W. Adams, Fred. Aldridge, A. B. Botts (who was also the jury foreman), William E. Bradley, Anthony Bush, Frank Beckwith, William E. Brent, Richard Brown and Daniel Davis, after hearing the evidence, found Sylvia Lucas not guilty.

SPENCE (1880)

THE VIRGINIA STAR of March 13, 1880 had a column heading sure to attract attention...

Murder.

STAFFORD COUNTY, VA, MARCH 9, 1880. The Stafford Store neighborhood was aroused early yesterday morning by the holding of a coroner's inquest and a post mortem examination on the body of a colored boy by the name of Oscar Spencer, where foul play was supposed to have been committed. The result of the inquest, under Justice R. G. Hickerson, acting coroner, and a thorough examination by Drs. Smoot and Bowen, revealed the fact that the boy, who was about twelve years of age, came to his death by the most brutal treatment at the hands of his mother, Amie Spencer. The coroner's warrant brought the body of the fiend in human shape before the Justice G. M. Weedon, who promptly committed her for trial.

You will be furnished with additional details of this un-precedented murder.

Snow is rapidly falling at this hour, 7 o'clock, a.m. "

On May 12 of that same year, the Stafford court overseer of the poor of the Rock Hill District was charged with binding out the two infant children of Amy Moore, AKA Spence, to William Payne of Fauquier County.

The practice of binding out was not as terrible as it sounds. Children whose parents were unable or unwilling to care for them were frequently sent to live with a foster family that was charged with feeding and educating the children. In addition, particularly in the eighteenth and the first half of the nineteenth century, this also included teaching the children a trade that would support them when they reached the age of adulthood, usually around 18 years old. Sometimes children or parents had some say as to who was to take the children. Frequently the courts made arrangements to place the bound-out children with families that were known to them as reliable and solvent. Court records show some names reoccurring over a number of years, suggesting that those families had several children in their care at a time. This system is very similar to the present day foster care system, with the exception of the family's requirement to teach the child a trade or skill.

This type of care is explained quite well in the June 12 guardianship hearing which stated that the children, Madison and James Moore, ages three and four, were to be treated well and given a common school education. The children were to remain with the Mistress Payne until they attained the age of 21 years.

There is a record of a marriage between Alexander Moore of Stafford County and Sally Payne, also of Stafford County, in 1882. This may indicate some relationship between the Moores and the Paynes that predated the marriage of these two, which may have included Amy and the family of William Payne of Fauquier (which county adjoins Stafford and has frequent liaisons with the northern area of Stafford County). Rock Hill District of Stafford adjoins Fauquier County. Moores' Corner is also in Rock Hill District, indicating a large number of Moore families living in that area of the District. The point of this is to show a possible connection of the Moore and Payne families, which could help explain why the William Payne family was chosen as guardian to Amy Moore's children. It is possible that William Payne may have been an uncle or cousin of Amy.

Had Amy Moore/Spence been providing a suitable environment to raise the children, they may have been returned to her when her prison term was over. However, the court probably took into consideration that the children's mother had been charged with killing their brother at approximately the same age that they would have been had they been returned to her care. Thus the charge to remain with the Paynes until they were 21.

Amy's trial came before Stafford County Court in *Commonwealth v. Amy Moore alias Spence* in July 1880. Her jury, consisting of O. P. Benson, John Anthon, Main Sthreshley [*sic*], Fred. G. Griffis, James Gill, Thomas Wilson, Mark Rodgers, William Black, James Woodard, William Menax, Charles Henry, and John M. Lee found her guilty of murder in the second degree. She was to be imprisoned for ten years.

Amy does not seem to have returned to Stafford County after her term of imprisonment was over.

Unneighborly Neighbors

STAFFORD COUNTY, VIRGINIA, was a rural community with a small population and families that were connected by marriages and property. In the early days, her younger sons were a part of the westward movement that settled the western sections of Virginia, and later Kentucky, Ohio and Indiana. But by the time of the American Revolution, the population of Stafford County had begun to stabilize.

Families living in proximity to each other often had children who married, thus forming bonds much in the manner of European royal dynasties. But if they did not marry, occasionally, proximity brought about antagonism.

FANT v. GRAVES (1793)

ON A SUNDAY in late February or early March 1793, George Stringfellow and Thomas Graves were walking together to Samuel Martin's. Fielding Fant walked after them with a gun in his hand. He remained about 30 steps away from them.

Fant didn't speak to either of them at that time. It seems apparent that there were bad feelings between Fant and Graves from an early date.

A while later, George heard Fielding tell Thomas that if ever he went through his field again, he would shoot him.[1]

Thomas Graves and Fielding Fant had a fight sometime before March 26, 1793. In that fight, Thomas had beaten Fielding and Fielding threatened Thomas that he would exact revenge for this beating.

Testimony from the court records picks up a parallel line of events that had some bearing on the murder.

Delphia Martin hired William Graves and his son, Thomas Graves, to repair her fence and put up a gate. At about three o'clock in the afternoon of March 26, 1793, Elias Fant was plowing the field next to her property, about 40 or 50 yards from her gate.

One witness saw Fielding walking about the field with something in his hand. Another witness, Delphia Martin, saw him walking with what appeared to her to be an ax in his hand. She heard him occasionally strike it against her fence.

While they were working on the gate, William told Thomas to bring him a stake, which he needed to continue the repairs. A few minutes later, William heard the sound of a commotion and saw Thomas fighting with Elias Fant. Immediately, Fielding ran up to the pair with an ax held in the position of striking. William immediately began to run toward the fighting pair. As he ran, he distinctly heard the sound of an ax hitting something. As he reached the pair, he saw his son, Thomas, struggling on the ground, bleeding badly from a wound in the head. Elias Fant had an ax in his hand. He swore that if anyone came near him he would serve them in the same manner.[2] There seems to be some confusion in the testimony about who had the ax, Elias or Fielding.

---

[1] Taken from the deposition of George Stringfellow Jr., Corporation Court of Fredericksburg

[2] Testimony taken from *Commonwealth v Fielding Fant*, Corporation Court of Fredericksburg

In the court held April 2, 1793, Fielding Fant of Brunswick Parish, Stafford County, a laborer, was indicted for assaulting Thomas Graves with an iron ax, hitting him in the head and causing him to die instantly.

Fielding Fant was the son of George Fant of Overwharton Parish in Stafford County.[3]   He came from a large family. George married and had seven children by his first wife. After her death he remarried and had ten children by the second wife. George died in Coles County, Illinois in 1839.

Fielding married Frances Hardin in about 1794.[4]   They had seven children, all born in Allen County, Kentucky. While there are no court records other than the indictment of this case, evidence suggests an outcome. The marriage of Fielding in the next year would indicate that Fielding was not convicted of the charges of murder. Since his first child, born in 1801, was born in Kentucky, Fielding must have left Stafford County soon after his marriage. Whether this was wanderlust or the desire to put the damaging effects of a murder accusation behind him is difficult to say for certain.

There seems to be some connection with the family of Evan Jones. The *Fant Genealogy*[5] lists George as the son of Evan Jones. Since the names and genealogy do not prove this as a blood relationship, it may be that he was an adopted or foster son of Evan Jones. Evan had other children, John Jones and James Crop. The different last name of James Crop may indicate a previous marriage of Evan's wife, or possibly an adoptive relationship.

George Jones, son of Evan Jones and of some kinship to Fielding Fant, was accused of the murder of Gerrard Stir in 1796   (See "Whodunit?" chapter).   Charges were later dropped. Evan Jones died about 1799.

---

[3] *Fant Genealogy* by Alfred E. Fant, printed privately in 1975
[4] Ibid.
[5] Ibid.

GRYMES v. GALLOWAY (1794)

A **POLITICALLY** and socially prominent family in the Rappahannock River area in its early years of settlement was the family of Grymes. Their social and political standing shielded them on at least two occasions from the full measure of the law.

Benjamin Grymes, Sr. was one of the justices in colonial Spotsylvania County. Along with Alexander Spotswood, Charles Dick and Fielding Lewis, he was among the highest-ranking leaders of the county. He was also "thoroughly disliked by almost everyone who had dealings with him. And time would prove him to be extravagant, incompetent and eventually, irrational."[6]

There are indications from newspaper articles in the *Virginia Gazette* in the late summer of 1771 that Grymes had been indicted, tried and found innocent of committing a murder, the victim unnamed. Grymes apparently was then charged with either packing the jury with "all my Mattapony friends" or bribing other justices and the coroner to manipulate their testimony to his advantage. (This last statement was a newspaper rebuttal issued by Grymes.)

This event was not the only problem that followed Benjamin Grymes Sr. "In the 1760's, Grymes sued almost everyone. Quite often he issued warrants to those who had treated him with 'disrespect as a justice.' He even issued such warrants to

---

[6] Paula Felder notes

other members of the court. On one occasion, when a victim of lesser stature was summoned to court and fined on the basis of Grymes' accusations, two members of the court promptly stood up as security for the man."[7.] Grymes was also brought before the Spotsylvania Court for abusing his wife. In 1768 he had turned the management of his estate over to Presley Thornton and his brother-in-law William Fitzhugh, at which time they pleaded for those indebted to Grymes' estate to settle with John Holliday so that they could pay off the debts of the estate.[8] By 1769 he had so antagonized the other Spotsylvania justices, the governor had him expelled from the Commission of the Peace. By 1772 his estate had gone into the equivalent of bankruptcy. In 1773 he put a notice in the paper that he and his family were moving to Mississippi by the fall of 1774. In 1774 the heirs of Philip Grymes, Esq. demanded of Benjamin Grymes that he give sufficient security to guarantee his future faithful administration of the estate and he was "enjoined from intermeddling in any manner or degree" in the said estate.[9]

By March 23, 1778, there is evidence that Grymes Sr. had died. A newspaper article states *"All persons who have any demands against the trustees of Mr. Benjamin Grymes, deceased, are requested to apply for payment to the subscriber who is now empowered to discharge them"* (signed by Anthony Thornton, Jr.)

---

[7] Taken, with permission, from the notes of Paula Felder

[8] Henry Fitzhugh was the only son of William Fitzhugh and grandson to William Fitzhugh the immigrant. Henry Fitzhugh married Lucy, daughter of Robert Carter. They had one daughter, Elizabeth, who married Benjamin Grymes in 1747 and who was the grandmother of Bishop Meade. The only son of Henry and Lucy was the William Fitzhugh mentioned here

[9] Philip was the eldest son of John Grymes and Lucy Ludwell of Middlesex County, Virginia. John's sons Philip, Benjamin and Ludwell and his daughters, Hannah (Potter), and Lucy (Burwell) were mentioned in his will dated 12 August 1747 with a codicil dated 4 October 1748. The will was probated 4 July 1749 in Middlesex County, VA. Taken from *The Virginia Historical Magazine*, Vol. 27, pp. 406-40

But the area could not breath a sigh of relief at the demise of Benjamin Grymes Sr. His son, Benjamin Grymes Jr., was on the scene and showing that he was his father's son in every sense of the word.

Grymes, Jr. was one of the young Fredericksburg men who were locally known to be hotheads. Later, because of the family's social standing, he and two other young men from this group were termed patriots for an event that was, to say the least, foolish. The event that occasioned this change of opinion occurred just prior to the Revolutionary War. The three young men impulsively rode to Williamsburg one night, and attempted to regain the gunpowder taken from the gunnery by the crown. Nothing ever came of their reckless ride. However, the family chose to view this as an act of patriotism, rather than the result of a night of drinking.[10]

Benjamin Grymes, the younger, was described as being 5'10" tall, handsome and well made (meaning a good physique). He seems to have had quite a few friends.

From notes of William Fitzhugh, there are indications that at some point in his early adulthood, Benjamin Grymes Jr. began exhibiting undesirable behavior, due in part to an excessive consumption of alcohol.

Eagles Nest, completed in 1686 by William Fitzhugh, was the ancestral home of the Fitzhugh and Grymes families. By 1701 the 55,000-acre plantation was the largest in colonial Virginia. Situated on the Potomac River, the construction and furnishings epitomized the wealth and prestige of the early families of Virginia's Northern Neck region. George Washington was said to have been a regular visitor to the home. This magnificent home was burned during one of Benjamin Grymes' Jr.'s poker parties in 1793.

But the greatest disgrace to the family was yet to come.

---

[10] This story comes from family tradition, letters of William Fitzhugh, and notes of Paula Felder.

Late in July 1794 there was a major scandal in Stafford/ Fredericksburg. The prominent merchant, Robert Galloway, was shot in cold blood and mortally wounded by Benjamin Grymes of Eagles Nest in Stafford County (now King George County) as Galloway rode past him on his way to Boyd's Hole. Timothy Green reported the shooting in great detail. Grymes had been hailing passers-by sociably but with the intent of committing mayhem. He had already made an attempt to shoot William Hooe. Later that same day, Galloway happened to ride past Eagles Nest. Grymes's aim seems to have improved after his attempts to shoot passers-by earlier in the day. Galloway was shot and died on the spot. Grymes was taken into custody and indicted for willful murder.[11] He was judged innocent by reason of insanity.

By November 11, 1794, Grymes had been taken to Eastern State Hospital in Williamsburg for evaluation. William Fitzhugh was left to manage Grymes' affairs during his confinement.

In an article in the *Virginia Herald* newspaper dated November 11, 1794, William Fitzhugh of Chatham states:

During the confinement of Mr. Benjamin Grymes, of Somerset, the management of his affairs must necessarily devolve on me; and as it is my wish to discharge all his just debts as fast as the money can be raised from the affairs intended for him and his family; I will thank his Creditors to furnish me with copies of their accounts as soon as they possibly can. It is also expected that those who are indebted to him will, without further application, pay up their balances.

On May 12, 1795, Elisha Hall, David C. Ker and Robert Wellford, practitioners of medicine, judged Benjamin Grymes Jr. to be a "person of disorderly mind."[12] He was committed to

---

[11] Taken, with permission, from Paula Felder's column, "The Way It Was," *The Free Lance Star*

[12] Notes of the Court of Directors Meeting for Eastern State Hospital. In the notes of Paula Felder.

the hospital where he stayed until sometime previous to March of 1796.

In a letter from William Fitzhugh to Benjamin Grymes (called "Ben" in the letter) after his release from the mental hospital, Fitzhugh warns Grymes of not making use of threats or an unguarded expression to anyone, even his enemies. He tells Grymes that "you will have the peace sworn against you, and you will be obliged to either go to jail or give security with a heavy penalty for your future conduct and be confined to your plantation. In this situation you can apply to no one but me, and as I am persuaded that every attempt would then be tried to make you forfeit your bail, in order to recover the penalty, which would end in the ruin of yourself and your family, it becomes you to conduct yourself in such a manner, as to prevent any such steps to be taken. You know by experience that you can do without spirituous liquor..."[13]

Grymes apparently gave some heed to his uncle's pleadings and did not find himself in jail for murder. In the settlement of his estate recorded in Fredericksburg, August 15, 1805, his wife, Sarah renounces all claim she has to the estate of her husband. Whether this is as a result of a legal maneuver or a prenuptial agreement, or if it is as a result of her attempt to distance herself from the man who brought her so much sorrow, can only be surmised.

---

[13] Copy of a letter from William Fitzhugh to Benjamin Grymes Jr. transcribed by Paula Felder.

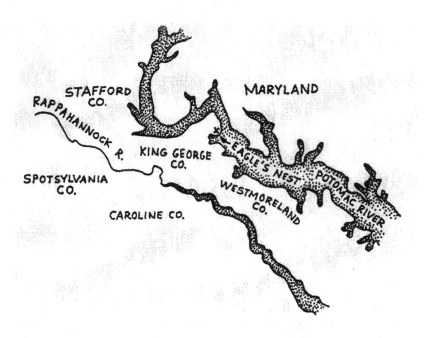

Rebuilt Eagles Nest, once home of the Grymes family

GATEWOOD v. HOPKINS (1805)

ANOTHER family that was well known in the area due to its land holdings and prolific offspring is that of Gatewood. The Gatewood family traces its lineage back to the early eighteenth century in Virginia's tidewater area. From there the family spread its branches, reaching Caroline County before the American Revolution. As with any family, the Gatewoods had their black sheep. Edmund Gatewood appears to have been one of those black sheep.

Court records do not indicate the cause of Edmund's dispute with Burton Hopkins. Earlier court records from Caroline County point to Edmund's problems managing money. He had become indebted to the estate of his father, Benjamin, by January 26, 1797. At that time Fleming Gatewood, Edmund's uncle, stated in a deposition that Edmund in 1790 acknowledged that he owed money to his father's estate.

Benjamin Gatewood was the son of James and Penelope Gatewood of Caroline County. James appears to have been quite prosperous. In 1783 his personal property consisted of 18 slaves, 8 horses and 16 cattle. Considering that the average person owned about one-quarter of that in Caroline County at that time, we can begin to form a picture of the social standing of that branch of the Gatewood family in its community.

When James Gatewood died sometime before 1793, he had already outlived his son, Benjamin. He named his son, Reuben, as his executor. By May 7, 1800, there was already dissension among his heirs about how the estate was divided. Caroline County chancery records show that upon the death of Penelope in 1794, family members began to squabble about the division of the land and slaves allotted to each other.

Edmund's aunt, Catharine (also known as Caty), married William Clarke, who proceeded to go through her money and then left her "to parts unknown." Depositions had him in the Fredericksburg jail in 1789 where he was met by a woman and child before leaving the area, never to be seen again. Caty gave Edmund her share of her father's estate on Christmas Eve, 1798.

Caty's brother, John, had already left for Kentucky in 1793, selling his part of James's bequest to Edmund. Edmund, in 1800, took his uncles Reuben and Richard to court to obtain an even larger part of the estate. In 1793 that estate was roughly described as a parcel of land on the south side of the Stage Road from Bowling Green to Burkes Bridge and bounded by Dejarnette on the north side and Thomas Burke to the south and the Mattaponi River.

How Burton Hopkins fits into this picture cannot be determined based on any surviving records. What we do know is that on November 8, 1805 in Caroline County, "Edmund Gatewood...shot recharged and shot forth feloniously, willfully and of his malice aforethought did strike, penetrate and wound giving to the said Burton Hopkins...with the leaden shot...discharged and shot forth out of the gun...in and upon the right side of the head of the said Burton Hopkins one mortal wound of the depth of one inch and of the breadth of one half an inch of which the said mortal wound the aforesaid Burton Hopkins...instantly dead."

Witnesses against Edmund included his neighbor, Joseph Dejarnette, as well as William Elliott, John Elliott, Benjamin Redd and Josiah Faulconer.

A murder indictment was brought against Edmund Gatewood in the Fredericksburg District Court in 1806. The jury consisted of Samuel Chiles, Henry Pitts, Robert Wright, Henry Wright, Gerrard Freeman, John Laughlin, John Turner, Thomas Buckner Jr., James Willson, Richard Bridges, Tarton W. Chiles and Thomas Broadus. He was convicted of murder in the second degree and sentenced to five years imprisonment in the penitentiary. Dated Friday, May 2, 1806. ☠

Murder in the Work Place

IN THE DARK YEARS at the end of the War Between the States, times were troubled, confused and constantly changing. The areas bordering the Rappahannock River saw major military action in the time between 1862 and 1865. Hardly a family in Fredericksburg or Spotsylvania was left unscathed by the battles that raged through the area. Stafford was, for all intents and purposes, occupied by Northern forces. Farms in all of the jurisdictions were scavenged for animals and foodstuffs. Everyday necessities were scarce. People were frightened and emotions ran close to the surface.

What is astonishing is that so few civilian-related murders occurred during this time. It may be because the civilians had seen so much bloodshed at their doorstep that they were willing to endure almost any insult, rather than have any further violence. However, there seemed to be an exception to this observation.

HARROW v. BOWLING (1864)

ONE MURDER occurred outside of a battle situation at the home of William Perry in Spotsylvania County.

The coroner's inquisition reads:

Spotsylvania County to wit An inquisition taken at the house of William Perry in the said county upon view of the body of James S.M. Harrow, there laying dead the jurors sworn to inquire when how and by what means the said James S.M. Harrow came to his death, upon their oaths do say that he was shot by a musket ball at the house of William Perry by R.W. Bowling. This is from the evidence before us.

In testimony whereof the said coroner and Jurors hereto set their hands this the 27th day of September 1864.

> *William W. Jones Coroner*
> *Jurors*
> *H. R. Robey, Foreman*
> *John G. Peyton, W. Mills, William A. White,*
> *George H. Proctor, A. D. Wroe(?),*
> *Walham Tabb, James Lewis, F. J. Ballard,*
> *J. H. Brook, A. J. Jett, P. Bowler*[1]

From the journal of Edward L. Heinichen, a confectioner from Fredericksburg who was a 2nd lieutenant in Company H, 2nd Battalion Virginia Reserves, we have this description of events:

There was at that time [previous to Feb. 1865] a young conscription officer by the name of James Harrow who ought to have been in the army and whose brutality was notorious. One of our men, W.B_____ came back from a five days furlough one day and told me "James Harrow has been shot and killed." said I, "did you do it?" Answered he "Would you blame me if I did?" I did not make any further inquiries.[2]

---

[1] Coroner's inquests Spotsylvania Circuit Court, Spotsylvania, VA
[2] Maryland Historical Society MS1860

A newspaper article that appeared in the *Christian Banner* in Fredericksburg in 1862 gives some idea of the sentiments that were present about the time that this murder took place.

> *We learn that the cowardly scoundrels are rendering themselves notoriously and eternally infamous by sneaking through the country during the dark hours of night and by violence, taking men from their homes, their wives and their children, and dragging them either into the army, or having them sent to Richmond for imprisonment, simply because they won't shout hosannas to Secession. There is an hour of terrible retribution awaiting such characters.*[3]

It may be behavior such as described in the article that gave James Harrow his reputation for brutality.

James S. M. Harrow enlisted as a private in the Confederate Army February 4, 1862. At the time, he lived in Stafford County. He enlisted for three years but was listed among the casualties "in the battles before Richmond" after a transfer to Purcell's Battery.[4] There is no further record of his service in the Confederate Army.

R. Wesley Bowling, accused of the murder of Harrow, was a young man of 25 or 26 at the time of Harrow's murder. He had been married at the beginning of the war on February 19, 1861, to Catherine A. Jett, who also lived in Spotsylvania. He was a farmer and seemed to have led a relatively peaceful life. His family had been in the Spotsylvania area for generations.

William Perry, in whose home the murder occurred, was about the same age as R. W. Bowling. He was also a farmer in Spotsylvania and had married Virginia Lancaster in 1860. A William Perry is listed among the members of Virginia's miltia.

In trying to piece together a complete picture from incomplete records a picture emerges, albeit somewhat fuzzily.

---

[3] *Christian Banner* dated May 17, 1862
[4] Compiled Service Records of the Confederate Army, Virginia units

James Harrow, who had been a member of Captain Cayce's Company of Light Artillery, utilized his well-known brutality to enlist R. Wesley Bowling in the Confederate Army. Bowling probably felt ambivalent about Virginia's secession from the Union and had tried to stay out of the conflict. Somehow he managed to avoid imprisonment or full time service in the Confederate Army. Probably as a compromise, he enlisted in the Virginia Reserves, which called for more of a defensive posture compared to the aggressive one enforced by the Army of Northern Virginia. While out on maneuvers, he obtained a five-day furlough. He went home to his young wife and friends. While at the home of his friend, William Perry, James Harrow came by and attempted to strong-arm either Perry or Bowling into joining the army. Bowling shot him, probably using the gun he had been utilizing for his reserves duty. Bowling left Perry's home and quickly returned to his unit where he casually mentioned Harrow's murder to one of the officers that he knew from the area. Perry, meanwhile, called the sheriff about Harrow's murder. He seemed to have no doubt about his innocence being evident. It seems probable that he also did not expect them to suspect his friend, Bowling, of the murder. Bowling was never arrested for Harrow's murder.

Fredericksburg was occupied by the Union Army immediately following the war and for the five years following the war. It is possible that this case was one that slipped through the cracks during the time of transition from civilian justice to military justice. Or, the Union occupation forces just may not have cared about one rebel killing another.

R. Wesley Bowling died in 1904 and is buried in Spotsylvania. His wife, Catherine A., is buried beside him, having died in 1897.

CAROLINE COUNTY still retains much of the rural charm that characterized it in the early nineteenth century. Farms cover the largest percentage of the county today. In 1808, almost the entire county was farmland. People led quiet lives. The social balance of the county was well established, with white farmers outnumbered by black slaves. Although the racial balance was not equal, we should not project 21st-century values and attitudes on the population of the 1800's.

Caroline County was one of the areas in Virginia that accepted racial intermarriages for much of the nineteenth century. It was not uncommon to find a black brother-in-law or sister-in-law at a family home, although at any formal function the strict racial segregation one would expect during that time period would have been observed.

As a result of this agrarian society and the relaxed attitude about race, very little tension was manifested in crimes of violence. While many court records for Caroline County are nonexistent due to destruction during the Civil War and other times, local newspapers and District Court records have very few mentions of criminal activity in Caroline County.

One of the few cases brought to light was the case of William Kirk and a black boy named Harry.

KIRK v HARRY (1808)

William Kirk was an elderly man living in Caroline County. He appears to have been living alone in 1808. At some point previous to April 24, Mrs. Caty Barby sent one of her servants, a young black boy named Harry, to live with Kirk.

At sunrise on the morning of April 25, 1808, William Kirk went to William Samuel, also of Caroline County, and told him that Harry had died of colic during the night and that he needed a coffin for him. Samuel went to his sister, Mrs. Caty Barby, to tell her of the death of Harry. Caty was certain that Harry had been murdered. What gave her that certainty was never stated. Nonetheless, because of her accusations, William Samuel and Caty Barby went to William Kirk's house and found Harry lying dead with a cloth wrapped around his head. Marks of violence covered his arms.

"Old man, the boy has certainly been murdered," said Samuel.

"I don't know that," replied Kirk.[5]

Samuel immediately went off to get someone to examine the boy. While he was gone, the boy was put into a coffin and brought to a hastily dug grave. Samuel arrived before Kirk could bury him and would not allow him to put the coffin into the grave until the boy's body had been examined.

Richard Saunders, McKenzie Beverley, William G. Sears and Lewis Upshaw examined the body of Harry, which had been brought to the plantation of McKenzie Beverley. There they discovered the real cause of death.

One wound went from the upper lip across the cheek and over the left eye. Another wound on the right temple went clear to the bone. Over the right eye, a third wound was about half an inch, and a fourth wound was at the edge of the hair above the right eye to the bone. The skin on the crown of the head was beaten loose from the skull for about five inches. Multiple smaller wounds covered his head and arms from the hand to the elbow.

The witnesses who acted as coroner's jury, testified that they went to Kirk's home and found a bloodied blanket and a poker from the fireplace covered in blood. Various parts of the house were covered with blood.

William Kirk was charged with the murder of Harry.

No other record of the case is found. ♀

---

[5] Deposition of William Samuel taken for the Virginia District Court

🕱 Murder Among Friends

HORSE RACES in Fredericksburg and in the counties of Virginia's Piedmont were well known from as early as the eighteenth century. People of all classes participated as jockeys. Everyone that attended made bets on the horses. Advertisements in newspapers of the eighteenth and early nineteenth century offered for sale or stud service horses that seem to have been known by name to the general population. Offspring of winning horses could also be found for sale. It should not be too surprising to note that Lexington, Kentucky, land of racehorses, was partially settled by people from this area of Virginia.

Emotions ran high at the horse races. Whether winning or losing, most people were in a heightened emotional state by the end of the day. The presence of alcoholic beverages only added to the potentially explosive atmosphere at these races.

HUGHLETT v. CARTER (1800)

SATURDAY, June 28, 1800, was a typical day at the races in Culpeper County. George Hughlett, John Popham and Thomas Thornhill had spent the day together, betting and drinking. Thomas Thornhill seemed particularly upset by his losses. Hughlett seemed to be in a jovial mood. Whether this was due to his winnings or the amount of alcohol he had consumed is debatable. In any event, Thornhill seemed touchy about Hughlett's conversation about the races that day. Later in a court deposition, Thornhill described that conversation:

"I told you to drop the subject! I played twice and I can't get any of my money back," Thornhill complained.

"Well, if you had played with honest men, you wouldn't have to worry about running anymore," Hughlett replied.[1]

John Carter, who apparently was a bystander during this conversation, seemed to take Hughlett's comments about betting with honest men personally.

"You're a damned rascal!" he spat out the words to Hughlett.

"If you say so again, I'll get you!" Hughlett replied.

"You're a damned rascal!" Carter reiterated.

Hughlett then raised his hand as if he were going to strike or grab Carter. Carter took his hand from his pocket, holding something made of iron. He lunged at Hughlett and immediately Hughlett cried out,

"I've been stabbed! I'm a dead man!"[2]

---

[1] Deposition of Thomas Thornhill, Fredericksburg District Court ID#568-87

[2] Ibid.

The noise of the argument attracted attention from all parts of the race ground. Thomas Walden heard of the report that a man had been stabbed by John Carter. Walden ran to where Hughlett lay. Carter was nowhere to be found. Walden left Hughlett to the attentions of others and ran to search out Carter. When he couldn't find him, he ran back to where Hughlett lay. Carter was standing by the deceased with his hands in his pockets.

"Did you kill him?" Walden questioned.

"No."

Immediately, Thomas Thornhill took a chisel from Carter's pocket and demanded to know why he killed Hughlett. Carter, apparently confused at the sight of the bloody chisel, replied that he had killed him with the chisel.[3]

Later, Carter was to deny that he ever said that he had killed Hughlett.[4]

Carter was brought to trial on July 4, 1800. The witness who saw Carter take the metal object from his pocket and stab Hughlett with it, John Lowen, did not appear at court. Probably as a result of the absence of this crucial witness, Carter was found not guilty.

---

[3] Deposition of Thomas Walden, Fredericksburg District Court ID#568-87

[4] Ibid.

CLARK v. YOWELL (1792)

THE SAGA of David Yowell and Nancy Clark, AKA Nancy Bryant, is as perplexing to us today as it undoubtedly was when it occurred in 1792. What is missing from the picture is the motive for the murder. Theories have circulated, one of which was that Nancy was pregnant with David's baby and told him of the pregnancy. This might explain why he then killed her and tried to kill himself rather than deal with the shame of the situation. There is no evidence that has been found to date, which actually gives a motive for this grisly murder, however.

Nancy Bryant, or Nancy Clark, as she was known in most of the court records, was the 15-year-old daughter of Elizabeth Clark. One of the few records we can find on this branch of the Clark family is that Elizabeth Clark was a legatee of William Golding, a schoolmaster of Culpeper who left a will in September 1771. This may be the same Elizabeth Clark that is listed as the daughter of James Clark, who wrote his will on June 2, 1789.

David Yowell Jr. was the husband of Elizabeth Berry and had six sons. He is believed to be the son of David Yowell Sr. of Culpeper County.

According to the *Virginia Herald* newspaper, "in the upper end of Culpeper County in Bromfield Parish, near Ragged Mountain, on Sunday evening last David Yowell murdered Nancy Carter who was about 15 years old at the time of her murder."[5]

In the presence of her mother, he stabbed her once, this cut not being mortal. Nancy's mother attempted to rescue her daughter. However, Yowell slashed the mother on her right

---

[5] *Virginia Herald* newspaper, October 11, 1792, Fredericksburg, VA

cheek to the bone. He then cut Nancy's throat in two places and split her left breast through to the bottom of her body, cut a gash along her right side, which let out her entrails and gave her several other wounds that proved mortal.

He then attempted to cut his own throat, severing his gullet and windpipe. Michael Klug [also spelled Klugg], a friend of David Yowell, was present during this violent attack and did nothing to aid Nancy or her mother.

David Yowell was taken under guard to his home to recover from his injuries until the time of his trial.

Yowell recovered from his wounds and by January 1793 was incarcerated in the Fredericksburg gaol. David apparently had friends who were concerned about his well-being. The friends may have even had hopes of getting him out of gaol. However, one of them, Michael Klugg (who had been present during the murder,) was observed visiting him outside of the gaol in January, giving him a small sum of money.[6] Whether Klugg's intentions were to give him the means to buy some necessity or to give him the means to pay off the gaoler as a means of escape is not known.

There was a rather bizarre newspaper statement, written anonymously, that warned the sheriff that there were some people who would like to see David Yowell set free and the sheriff needed to keep a sharp watch on his prisoner.[7]

David Yowell was convicted of the murder of Nancy Clark, also known as Nancy Bryant, age about 15 years old.

In March 1793, Yowell filed an appeal. The justification given for the appeal was, incredibly, that Nancy's wounds were not sufficient to cause death and that the place named as the site of the murder was not included in the indictment.

Elizabeth, concerned that at least two of the witnesses had "taken a journey to the Southern country" and that there would not be sufficient evidence to reconvict Yowell, sent a note from her home in Madison County to the Fredericksburg

---

[6] *Virginia Herald* newspaper January 17, 1793
[7] Ibid.

District Court, listing witnesses that included Michael Klug, who would be able to testify for the Commonwealth against Yowell. [8]

In April, 1793, Michael Klugg was indicted as an accessory to the murder of Nancy Clark. Mann Page, foreman of the jury, returned the indictment with the determination, "not a true bill" indicating that the jurors did not feel there was sufficient evidence to convict Klugg as an accessory to murder. [9]

On September 29, 1793, one day short of a year after Nancy Clark's death, David Yowell was scheduled to appear before the District Court for his appeal.[10] But, instead, a brief notice appeared in the newspaper.

The Court for the District of Fredericksburg was on Monday last, opened at the Court House in this town before the honorable Judges Henry and Tazewell. David Yowell, who has been confined for nearly a year in the gaol of this town for the murder of Nancy Clark, died on Monday last on the day which his trial was to take place.[11]

---

[8] Letter from Elizabeth Carter to the Fredericksburg District Court

[9] *Commonwealth v Klug,* Fredericksburg District Court record #387-74

[10] *Commonwealth v Yowell,* Fredericksburg District Court record #387-87

[11] *Virginia Herald,* October 3, 1793

GRAYSON v. NOEL (1924)

"THORNTON GRAYSON, colored pool room operator of this city [Fredericksburg] is at liberty on a bond of $5,000, charged with the murder of Caesar Noel, another Negro, following the latter's death with tetanus Sunday night as a result of an injury alleged to have been inflicted by Grayson on the night of May 15 [1924].

"No report of the fracas was made to police until Saturday, when lockjaw set in and Noel's physicians reported there were but slight chances for his recovery. Justice A. G. Billingsley went to the colored man's home on Wolfe Street Saturday evening and recorded his dying declaration, in which Noel named Grayson as his assailant. Grayson was arrested and bailed Saturday night for the sum of $1000 for his appearance in police court Monday morning. Owing to Noel's death Sunday night, Grayson's bond was increased to $5000 by Justice J. M. H. Willis Monday morning when Messrs. F. W. Coleman and W. W. Butzner, counsel for the accused, requested bail until Thursday, May 29, at 9 a.m. when a preliminary hearing will take place in police court.

"According to information in the hands of the authorities, a party of five Negroes, Thornton Grayson, Early Scott, William H. Carter, Jim alias Ison Williams and Eddie Lucas, were invited by Caesar Noel to the home of his sister, Louise Noel, for a craps game on the night of May 15. Noel is alleged to have sold the crowd a pint of liquor for $2 and later treated with another pint. A blanket was spread on the floor of the dwelling on Wolfe Street near the intersection of Princess Anne, dice were produced and gambling ensued. According to witnesses, Grayson accused Noel of cheating and an altercation followed, during which the pair was parted by the other men.

The craps game was resumed only to be interrupted again when Noel was charged with playing unfair by another of the group. Noel, it was said, then ordered the men from the house and picked up a club. During the scuffle Grayson is alleged to have struck Noel on his left check with a glass bottle, inflicting a wound which later developed tetanus, and from which death resulted at 10 p.m. Sunday."[12]

---

[12] *Free Lance* newspaper, May 26, 1924, Fredericksburg, VA

Alum Spring in 1998, a walkway by the spring

💀 Duels at Alum Spring

DUELING in the United States was illegal after the American Revolution, although it was occasionally used (with noteworthy examples being Aaron Burr v Alexander Hamilton and Andrew Jackson) to settle disputes. While dueling was seldom utilized as a method of argument in the Virginia Piedmont, there are a few examples of its occurrence. Since it was illegal, the arrangements and events of a duel were secretive. The only accounts we have are from eyewitnesses and occasional records.

Benjamin Henry Latrobe visited Alum Spring on July 24, 1796. He described the rock ledge as a freestone (sandstone) or coarse grit with a great quantity of quartz and granite pebbles. He noted the petrified wood fossils and the holes and impressions of the former carbonized wood now weathered away. Mention was made of the edges of the rock being coated with crystals of alum and he described the whole situation as "beautifully romantic."

GLASSELL v RITCHIE (1790)

WHEN writing of his travels in Virginia in the summer of 1791, the Frenchman Ferdinand M. Bayard noted the Americans were imprudent imitators of the English, especially in regards to dueling with pistols. There was much talk of a recent one and he thought it strange the magistrates did not prosecute these violators of the law.

The timing and place of his writing make it likely he was referring to the duel of two Fredericksburg businessmen the year before which had taken place at Alum Spring.

By reconciling the account of the duel as recorded by Robert Reid Howison from published portions of his autobiography with a letter of April 3, 1790 from Henry Lee to James Madison, and with the identified Spotsylvania court records, the events may have been as follows.

In or about March of 1790 the members of the Masonic Lodge #4 of Fredericksburg gave a large and brilliant ball. Among those in attendance were members William Glassell and Robert Ritchie.

William Glassell, a native of Scotland, was a successful merchant and respected citizen who had married a sister of Anthony Buck, the latter a highly esteemed auctioneer in the town. Glassell had escorted to the ball a young, attractive and respected orphan girl who was living in his home.

Mr. Ritchie was originally from Essex County down the river from Fredericksburg, but he had been doing business in the town. He was not married. During the course of the evening at the Masonic Ball, and somewhat under the influence of wine, Ritchie offered a distinct insult to Glassell's young guest, then refused to make a suitable apology when called upon to do so.

Glassell sent a formal challenge, which Ritchie accepted, choosing pistols as the weapons and Alum Spring as the place. Ritchie, knowing Glassell to be an excellent marksman, was concerned enough over the event to make his will which was dated March 27, 1790 and if probated, left all his legacy to his sister, Elenora.

William Glassell had second thoughts and through friends, attempted to get Ritchie to reconsider. Ritchie refused and the duel took place on the pathway along the Alum Spring road in front of the clear mill pond.

At first shot, Ritchie fell to the ground. Glassell hurried to his side and implored forgiveness, which was refused.

After Ritchie's death, a murder warrant was issued. Glassell was arrested and taken before a magistrate, but was acquitted.[1]

THORNTON v CONWAY (1803)

THE END of the year 1803 marked another tragedy at Alum Spring, the Thornton-Conway Duel.

William Thornton was born September 24, 1772 at a Stafford County farm, downriver from Fredericksburg and nearly opposite "Nottingham," the home of John Spotswood. William's father, John Thornton, had died and his mother, Catherine, had married Dr. Robert Wellford, whose home at 1501 Caroline Street in Fredericksburg still stands.

---

[1] The story of the Glassell v Ritchie duel was taken from *Alum Spring Park*, unpublished manuscript by Robert Hodge, Fredericksburg, 1971.

The 21-year-old William had a cousin, Francis Fitzhugh Conway, of nearly the same age. The Conways reportedly were a prominent Caroline County family living at Mount Zion.

These two cousins were each attracted to a young niece of James Madison (the man who would in 1808 become the fourth President of the United States). Miss Nellie Madison was a Christmas holiday guest at Chatham in this year of 1803. Chatham was the lovely home of the Fitzhugh family overlooking the Rappahannock River in Stafford County.

Chatham in May 1863. *Photo taken by Timothy H. O'Sullivan*[2]

Nellie was most likely a friend of William Fitzhugh's 20-year-old daughter, Ann Randolph, who was also known as Nancy. Nellie, for two years had been the guest of Mrs. William Craik and/or the guest of 15-year-old Mary Lee (Mollie) Fitzhugh.

---

[2] *Selected Civil War photographs 1861-1865* Library of Congress Collection of Photographs

The two cousins, William and Francis, arrived at the Chatham festivities on horseback and their horses were stabled. Francis had adorned his horse with a brand-new, handsome bridle (a Christmas gift?) and during the evening made veiled references to Miss Nellie as to the "surprise" he would reveal later that evening (hoping, of course, to win her favor!)

Unfortunately, when departure time came and Francis was primed to "show off" his new bridle, the groom had switched bridles on the horses and it was William's horse that made the greatest impression on Miss Nellie.

The hurting Francis accused William of having bribed the groom. The denial simply aggravated the argument and the end result was a challenge to a pistol duel to take place at the Alum Spring Mill site.

The parents were not made aware of the impending duel, but on that Monday morning at the breakfast table Mrs. Conway was distressed as she recounted a dream in which she vividly saw a man on a white horse hastening to her house with a message that her son was dead.

On that same morning, William Thornton, with his half-brother, John Spotswood Wellford serving as his second, and Francis Fitzhugh Conway met on the narrow pathway between the Alum Spring rock and the millpond. At the word "fire," both shots sounded almost simultaneously and each bullet passed through the region of the bladder in each combatant.

Thornton was able to ride back to Fredericksburg where Dr. Wellford admitted that the wound would be fatal. Thornton's death occurred on Tuesday at the same hour that Francis Conway died.

That Tuesday afternoon, a man riding a white horse rode up to the home of Francis Conway and informed his mother of her son's death.

The *Virginia Herald* of February 17, 1804 carried a notice that a brace of brass-barreled pistols was found near the Alum Springs and could be claimed from William or John Rutter. 💀

💀 Holding A Grudge

FLINCH v. NEWTON (1877)

STAFFORD COUNTY, in the nineteenth century, was not a community hardened by numerous acts of violence. Although the community was an old one, dating back to the 1600's, it had maintained its rural character. The population consisted mainly of farmers and merchants, occasionally with a blacksmith or carpenter. While some counties with that early of a beginning had increased in population over the years, Stafford still had a sparse number of people.

Large farms that had been in the same families for generations, fields that lay fallow, and large tracts of undisturbed woods spread the population thinly. The largest concentration of people resided in Falmouth, a tiny port town clinging to the banks of the Rappahannock River.

James Finch or Tayler Flinch—he was known by both names—was born about 1866, probably in Alexandria, VA. Who his parents were or what happened to them is not known. If James/Tayler knew, he never told anyone. He had drifted down from Alexandria, about 25 miles north of Stafford, and floated around the county as a sort of waif, earning a livelihood by working at odd jobs in a neighborhood, then going on to another. Today we would categorize him as a homeless child.

As might be expected from an eleven-year-old child who was basically raising himself, his habits and language were not appropriate for most kinds of people, even the rather laid-back farmers of a small southern community. His constant use of profanity was found so offensive by at least one parent that he forbade his children to associate with James/Tayler. That parent was William B. Newton.

The Newtons were a family whose roots were firmly planted in the misty beginnings of Stafford County. Some branches of the family even had heritage in the Indian tribes that lived in Stafford before the time of John Smith.

William and Virginia Newton were owners of a small farm that was connected to the much larger farm of Virginia's mother, Susan Potts. There were at least two children in 1877, Paul, age nine, and Silas, age seven. A brother or cousin, George, and his wife and children lived down the street from them.

For some reason, James Finch took it into his head to associate with one of the few people he was forbidden to see. As Paul Newton was walking to school on Friday, April 27, 1877, James asked to go into the Newton's house. Paul, knowing his father's prohibition against Finch, told him no. Finch, angered at this refusal, said "I'll fix you when you come on back!"[1]

On his way back from school that day, Paul and his younger brother passed James Finch, who was sitting on a log beside the road. Just as he passed, Finch raised the gun he was holding and shot the nine-year-old boy in the back, near the shoulder blade.[2] The bullet tore a large hole through his body. Paul died. Finch declared that he had only been trying

---

[1] *Virginia Star* newspaper May 2, 1877, Fredericksburg, VA
[2] Ibid.

to frighten Paul. However, witnesses testified that after shooting Paul, James went to the body and looked down at it for a moment. He then took the gun he had been carrying and put it away in the Newton house. He returned to the body of the little boy, looked at it intently then ran into the pine woods.

James apparently ran through the woods until he reached Sim Peyton's farm. Constable Bloxton, of the Stafford sheriff's office, found him Saturday. Finch made no comment to Peyton about the murder. In the days before radio and television, it is not surprising to learn that Mr. Peyton knew nothing about the murder until Bloxton came looking for Finch. James Finch, also known as Tayler Flinch, was arrested and arraigned before the local magistrate. He was then put in jail until his trial.

That trial occurred rapidly. During the June (1877) term of the Stafford Court it was determined that Tayler Flinch (as he became known in the court records) was a pauper and unable to afford an attorney. The court appointed John H. Suttle and John T. Goolrick as his attorneys. The prosecuting attorney for the Commonwealth was Commonwealth Attorney Judge J. B. Jett. Goolrick later became a Fredericksburg Court judge. He also authored a book, *Historic Fredericksburg, The Story of An Old Town,* a sentimentalized version of Fredericksburg's history.

At his arraignment Tayler was charged with murder in the first degree. His plea at his court date of June 20 was not guilty. The case was continued to the next day.

According to the law at the time, there is a presumption only of malice in criminals between the ages of seven and fourteen. This may be rebutted by testimony. The jury, as usual, determined the degree of premeditation and malice.

Records of the testimony at the trial, unfortunately, no longer exist in Stafford. Newspaper coverage only states that the trial promised to be a very interesting one to the legal community. It seems that a murder committed by one so young was unprecedented in that portion of the state.[3]

The jury, after hearing the testimony, found Tayler Flinch guilty of murder in the second degree. He was sentenced to eleven years in the penitentiary. The jury foreman asked the court to set aside the verdict of the young murderer and grant him a new trial. What motivated the same jury that convicted the child of murder to request the judge to set aside their verdict and grant the defendant a new trial will have to remain a mystery. The court refused the jury foreman's request for a new trial. James Finch/Tayler Flinch went to the penitentiary. There is no further indication of him in census records for the state of Virginia.

KENDALL v POWELL (1924)

"**WITH** a huge throng of spectators from several counties besieging the historic little courthouse at Spotsylvania, argument of the case of Commonwealth vs. Chas. B. Kendall was begun Tuesday afternoon..."[4]

The beginning of the Kendall trial for the murder of Robert Llewellyn Powell was as dramatic as the actual story of the murder.

---

[3] Ibid.
[4] *Free Lance*, September 4, 1924, Fredericksburg, VA

Charles Broadway Kendall was born 7 December 1899 to Annie B. and Julian F. Kendall. At the time of his birth he had three older sisters, Mary (born August 11, 1893), Ann Meredith (born about 1896) and Roberta (born about 1898). Later, three other sisters would follow, Julia F. (born October 10, 1902), Lindsay (birthdate unknown), and Betty B. (born October 21, 1907).[5] Charles was a fresh-faced young man with ruddy cheeks and blue eyes. He was slim, weighing about 130 pounds.

Robert Llewellyn Powell was born August 30, 1886 to James L. Powell and Caroline Elizabeth Jones.[6] One of Robert's brothers was S. Peter Powell, an attorney who was elected as Commonwealth Attorney in 1924. His other brothers were James L. (who moved to Muskogee, Oklahoma), John (who moved to Denver, Colorado) and William (both of Chicago, Illinois). Robert also had three sisters, Orlene (who married Mr. Biggs), Elsie (who moved to Washington, D.C.) and Julia (who married Mr. Heigh of Washington, D.C.)[7]

Spotsylvania County is situated in eastern Virginia with the Rappahannock River forming its northeastern border. Until the 1980's it was a rural county with slightly rolling hills, farms and wooded areas. In the first decade of the twentieth century a young doctor set up practice in the county whose name was Robert Llewellyn Powell. His family was well known in the county, having resided here for generations. Two things were known about him, personally: he was well liked by his patients and there were persistent rumors of his romantic involvement with various attractive Spotsylvania females.

He was an attractive man. He was also a large man, weighing about 200 pounds with a large, muscular build.

---

[5] Tombstones at Mt. Hermon Baptist Church, Caroline County, Virginia

[6] Powell family cemetery at Granite Springs, Spotsylvania County, Virginia

[7] *Free Lance*, May 18, 1924

DR. ROBERT L. POWELL

While he was liked by his patients and seemed to have an interest in women, he remained a persistent bachelor. He told one young lady that he would not marry until his mother died.

Another time, a woman believed his mother was planning to leave him the family home if he married her. Local matchmakers were continually coupling his name with one or another of eligible young ladies. But as years passed and Dr. Powell remained a bachelor, residents eventually gave up.

In 1919 Robert became ill with pneumonia.[8] One of his sisters' friends, Ann Meredith Kendall, took time to help nurse him while he was ill. She read to him, sat and talked to him and at times, helped feed him. At one point, certain that death was near, Robert begged Meredith to pray for him, for he declared, he did not know how to pray. She prayed for him then, and continued to pray for him after his recovery.

By January of 1920 Robert had recovered from pneumonia. It was then that the confirmed bachelor, realizing the worth of the selfless young lady who nursed him back to health, asked Meredith to marry him.

Ann Meredith Kendall was a young lady who was also well known in the countryside. Her family had lived in Spotsylvania for several generations and was a part of the county government, her uncle, Clarence Jones, having been the head of the Board of Supervisors. She was the second of nine children. In 1920 she was 24 years old and had a job teaching school in West Point, Virginia. Her younger brother, Charles Broadway Kendall, had just turned twenty and his father had turned a part of the family farm over to him to manage.

In person Meredith was described as slim and pretty. She displayed a forthright and honest personality. She was naive in the ways of love and trusted everyone. She had known of Robert for years, the two families residing within two miles of each other. But it was only after both had matured that she began to see him as someone other than the older brother of her playmates. There was some discrepancy in age, he being

---

[8] All dialog and situations come from the newspaper transcript of the trial. Newspapers that covered the story locally were the *Free Lance* and the *Virginia Star*

thirty-three and she only twenty-four; but other than that respect, there was no possible objection from either family. The engagement was in January. However, by November of 1922, no plans for the wedding of the couple had been announced.

Rumors began filtering back to Meredith that Robert had been seen with other women. The rumors persisted. Near the end of November, Meredith spoke to Robert's mother, expressing her concerns.

"Robert can't be depended upon, Meredith. I don't think he is true." Mrs. Powell's words only confirmed what Meredith had suspected for a while.

That day, Meredith spoke to Robert for a long time. Robert was seen to be greatly agitated.

The little schoolteacher went back to teaching her class after Thanksgiving, sadder, but resolved to do the right thing. Meredith was one of those naturally nurturing women who thought she could make people's lives better if she just tried hard enough. Although at first it was an emotional challenge, Meredith tried to remain friends with Robert, writing letters to him while she was away at her teaching job and maintaining friendly relationships with his sisters and mother.

Meredith's summer vacations were spent at her parents' home in Spotsylvania County. Robert continued to visit the family, more frequently when Meredith was home.

One night during the summer of 1923 Robert came over to visit the Kendall family. Several hours passed in pleasant conversation. When the evening came to a close, Meredith walked Robert to the door. As they stood out on the porch saying goodbye, Robert grabbed Meredith's arm and tried to pull her to him. Meredith fought him and broke away, running back into the now darkened home. Robert left.

In July of that same year, Robert again came to visit the Kendalls. Although she had become wary of Robert's motives after the previous incident, his charming manner and apparent good will toward the family put her back at ease in his presence.

About 11:30 that night, the family members had retired for the evening and Robert was preparing to leave. Meredith again walked him to the door. Robert grabbed her roughly around the waist and restrained one of her hands, pulling her to him. After a brief scuffle, Meredith again broke away from him, but her previous fears about him had been re-ignited. Telling him to leave, Meredith resolved to have nothing more to do with him.

Robert persisted in visiting the Kendall home, however. When Meredith happened to be present, he paid lavish attention to Meredith's younger sister Julia. Julia was only twenty years old.

In September, Charles, Meredith's brother, brought her to the train station in Fredericksburg to catch the train to her West Point teaching job. Charles, as the eldest of the three Kendall brothers, had begun to assume more and more of the family responsibilities. Most of the family farm had been turned over to him by 1923. His sisters also began turning to him in times of trouble. He acted as their mediator with their parents and as the "court of first appeal" when they were in trouble. Although he was younger than Meredith, she still turned to him to help her with something that had been troubling her since July.

"Charles, I want you to watch out for the younger girls," she told him.

"Of course I will. Don't I always?" he replied, smiling fondly at her.

"No, I mean, you need to protect them from Dr. Powell. I have been with him and I know him," she insisted.

Charles, bewildered by her insistence, agreed.

Meredith again resumed her correspondence with Robert Powell, or Bob, as she knew him to be called. His letters became more despondent. He complained about being bored, tired of the work routine. He told her he thought about quitting his practice and leaving for parts unknown.

However, in October, 1923, Robert Powell, age 37, began seeing Meredith's sister, Julia, who was age 20. They met at

Julia's married sister's house because of the disapproval that their relationship drew from Charles and Julia's mother. Mary Young, however, was not at all pleased about the attention Robert was paying to her little sister. She complained to their mother that they were meeting at her house and Powell could not keep his hands off Julia.

At election time, Charles was asked to be a judge during the election, making certain that voters were registered and had paid their taxes, making them eligible to vote. Robert Powell came to vote, escorting Myrtle Eustace Dulin, the pretty young wife of the storekeeper, Lewis Dulin. Charles was speechless, not because Dr. Powell was seeing a married woman, but because he was seeing the married woman that Charles himself had been seeing!

Disillusioned and frustrated, Charles decided it was best for him to leave the area. He borrowed $40.00 from his uncle, Clarence Jones, and left to find work in Pittsburgh, Pennsylvania.

At Christmas time, Meredith returned home for vacation. While there she paid a visit to the Powell home. Robert's brother, Peter, had just been elected Commonwealth Attorney for Spotsylvania County. Meredith congratulated him on his win.

"My mother was sorry that Charles had not paid their taxes. Because of that, she was not able to vote for you at this election."

Robert overheard their conversation. "The little scoundrel, he didn't want you to vote for Peter," he hissed.

A while later, Meredith had the opportunity to speak to Robert privately. She had been hearing rumors that he had been seeing Leslie Chewning, who was separated from her husband, and also Mrs. Faulkner. It was not in his best interest to be seeing married women, she felt.

"Charles Kendall is lying on me and I am getting damned tired of it, and damn you, you are no better then those who are lying on me!" he shouted at her. "You keep on.

Something is going to happen to your family to stop you all from talking and I'll be glad of it!"

Robert, because of his job as a physician, was knowledgeable about a private matter involving a Kendall family member. Meredith, unaware of what he was talking about, left.

Roberta, one year older than Charles, was the third daughter of Julian and Annie Kendall. She had been dating Emmett Taylor for about five years. Roberta had just seen Robert Powell, as a doctor, and had him confirm that she was pregnant. He had prescribed a drug called ergot, one of several that had been given to women for several female related problems in the past but had lately fallen into disfavor because of the problems it had caused with side effects, one of which was to cause abortions.

Roberta took the drug, which made her deathly ill, but did not cause the baby to abort. She did not recover from this drug-induced illness until January. She returned to Dr. Powell and reported that she was still pregnant. He gave her a letter that would admit her to a maternity hospital in Tennessee where she was told she could "get rid of it." Roberta decided she did not want to go.

By early April her condition had reached the phase where she was not able to hide her pregnancy any longer.

Charles, in the meantime, had come home to visit his family for Easter. All seemed to be going well. All of his sisters had stopped seeing Dr. Powell. The farm was doing well. No one seemed to have any major crisis.

Then Roberta left a note on Charles' dresser, telling him about her pregnancy and asking him to intercede for her with their parents. When asked why she didn't tell Charles in person, she sobbed that she was too embarrassed by her situation to tell him face to face. Charles came to her immediately and told her not to worry. He would talk to their parents.

Julian Kendall, furious at Roberta and Emmett for their indiscretion, took action.

"Charles, do you have a gun?" he asked his eldest son.

"No."

"Well, I want you to get one," he snapped. Charles did as his father ordered. The two of them went looking for Emmett Taylor.

Once the pair found Emmett, they brought him, at gunpoint, to the Kendall home. There he stayed through the night, sitting in the living room, guarded by a furious father and an indignant brother. At sunrise the next morning, Emmett, Roberta, Charles and Julian went to the courthouse. Emmett and Roberta were married on the spot. As soon as he was married, however, Emmett left and refused to live with Roberta. A child was born on July 15, 1924.

Roberta's wedding did not make things better. Mrs. Kendall, while cleaning her daughter's room, discovered the bottle of ergot. When asked why she had this drug, which Mrs. Kendall was familiar with, Roberta went on to explain how she had gone to see Dr. Powell. Infuriated, Mrs. Kendall told Charles about the drug. Charles decided not to go back to Pittsburgh. A most unfortunate decision.

About a month later, Charles spent Thursday, May 14, running errands. About six o'clock that evening he went to Dulin's store. Myrtle was alone at the store. They went to one of the upstairs rooms for about 20 minutes, then Charles left. He visited Vernie Graves, and then went to Louisa County, which is adjacent to Spotsylvania County. At eight or nine o'clock that night, he returned to Dulin's store. He said he was supposed to meet G. W. Briscoe at the store. As he entered, he saw Myrtle and Dr. Powell there. Robert came toward Charles.

"Charles, you've been lying on me long enough and I'm damned tired of it; and I heard that you said you were going to riddle my body with bullets."

Charles replied, "I heard that you were going to mash my face, and whoever said it told a damn lie."

Myrtle Dulin, seeing where this kind of talk was leading, pleaded with the two men to leave the store so there would not be any trouble in the store while Mr. Dulin was away. Charles asked Robert to go outside so that they could settle their difficulty without damaging the store. Powell turned and struck Charles. He beat him around the head so badly that Charles never had the chance to hit back, falling to the floor unconscious after having his face mashed.

Regaining consciousness, Charles left the little store and went to Aunt Louisa Comfort's home. There she washed the blood from his face and helped him get cleaned up. He went back to Dulin's, finding no one there but Mrs. Dulin and G. W. Briscoe, the person he was supposed to meet previously. The two men went to Louisa County and spent the hours drinking, returning to Dulin's at about 2 A.M. Briscoe picked up his car and the two men went home.

Three days passed in relative peace. The last hours of peace ended a little after three o'clock. Charles Kendall met his sister, Julia, at Mine Run. After a brief conversation, he left to run some errands. His first stop was Dulin's store to buy gas and a bag of salt. Dr. Powell was at the store. Kendall apparently managed to avoid meeting with Powell for a few minutes. The he heard Powell state that it was time that he was going. As Powell left the store, Kendall turned and said he would like to speak to him about a private matter. Could he meet him down the road?

"All right, sir. I'll be right down." Powell replied. Kendall's stated intent was to ask Powell for an apology for insulting his two sisters, for giving his sister Roberta the illegal abortion medicine, for accusing Kendall of lying and for beating him. Kendall seemed reluctant to discuss his sisters' situations in front of anyone, including his former heartthrob, Mrs. Myrtle Dulin. He also may have been worried about being beaten up again in front of Mrs. Dulin.

Kendall parked his car on the dirt road at the fork in the main road. Powell drove up and parked his car about ten feet away from Kendall's.

"You treated my sisters dirty, you accused me unjustly and you beat me up. I think you ought to apologize."

"I beat you the other night and I guess I can finish it now," Powell replied.

Powell started to move toward Kendall. He backed up about 20 yards and told Powell to stop. Powell kept coming towards him.

"If you take another step I will shoot you!" Kendall yelled.

Powell cursed him and told him he wouldn't shoot anybody. He took another step and Kendall fired.

Powell whirled around and began to run between the two cars. Thinking he had missed him and that Powell had a gun in his car, Kendall shot again. Powell yelled and fell to the ground. Kendall shot four more times, only two of the shots hitting Powell.

Ennis Pemberton, his mother Nellie and Pat Sullivan were driving in Pemberton's truck along the road near the fork where Powell and Kendall were. Pemberton saw Kendall shoot Powell. Massie V. Harris heard the first shot. He looked down the road where the sound of the shot came from and saw Kendall with pistol in hand advancing on and shooting at Powell. He then watched Kendall run to his car, crank it and drive away.

Harris ran to Powell and found him lying on his side, bleeding profusely. Powell, in great pain, asked someone to get his mother and brother Peter. Harris's daughter, Agnes ran to the scene. Powell said he wanted to make a dying statement. Agnes wrote, "I believe I am dying. I cannot live. I was shot by Charles Kendall." G. W. Briscoe, Peter White and Bunk Murphy ran up to see what had happened. Briscoe, closest to Powell heard him say "The boy didn't treat me fair. I don't reckon I treated the boy right and am sorry for it."

Harris and Pemberton, who had stopped his truck and run over to assist, made a stretcher out of a blanket and took the wounded man to Harris's house. Powell's mother and sister Orlene arrived at the Harris house soon after the men got Powell inside. They were with him when, at about 6 o'clock, Robert Llewellyn Powell died. Peter arrived just minutes before his brother died, too late to take him to the hospital where Peter had been frantically trying to arrange medical help.

After driving from the scene of the murder, Charles passed a friend of his, Arthur Raines, on the road to Louisa County. Arthur got in the car with him and they drove to the Trevillians station. Along the way, Kendall related what had happened to Arthur. The two men boarded a westbound train. When they arrived in Cincinnati, Ohio, Raines managed to convince Kendall to return home and turn himself over to the sheriff. Two hours after arriving in Cincinnati, the two were on an eastbound train, returning to the Orange County station. There they hired a liveryman to drive them as far as the improved road went. From there they began to walk home. At this point, Orange County Sheriff Selby drove by and immediately recognized Kendall. Not realizing that Arthur had nothing to do with the shooting, Selby took both men into custody.

Charles immediately told the sheriff that Raines was an innocent party. Selby held Raines for a day or so, checking out Kendall's story. When he determined that there were no charges pending against Raines, he let him go. However, the whole experience was too traumatic for Arthur Raines. When he arrived home, he took his gun and shot himself in the head.

Charles Kendall was tried for first-degree murder in August 1924. The trial drew throngs of people from the surrounding counties. The courthouse was packed every day of the trial. At times children were excluded from the courtroom. At other times, women were dismissed. And not to be biased, there were even times when the men were cast out of the packed courtroom.

Pre-trail publicity that was extremely one-sided against Kendall and several legal improprieties forced the defense to move for a change of venue.[9] While that was not granted, the court did allow the jury to be selected from Charlottesville and Alexandria.   Considering that a large portion of the county was related in one form or another to either the Kendalls or the Powells, that seemed to be a minimal legal precaution to assure a fair trial.

CHARLES E. KENDALL.

---

[9] Taken from the court papers in the Spotsylvania Circuit Court in the case of *Commonwealth v Kendall*

On September 6, 1924, the *Free Lance* newspaper headline read:

KENDALL ACQUITTED OF MURDER CHARGE;
verdict of Not Guilty is reached
in Powell Slaying Case after Jury is out Seventy Minutes.
Accused Returns Home With Family.

After the verdict, friends surrounded the Kendalls, shaking hands and congratulating the freed man and his sobbing sisters. For nearly an hour after the acquittal, groups of men and women hung about the courtyard, discussing the verdict. The majority of expressions were of great surprise. Immense crowds have followed the trial in Spotsylvania Circuit Court through its nine sensational days, with the record breaking number in attendance on the final day. No man, many say, ever owed more to a mortal the Charles Kendall owes to his sister Ann Meredith. The appealing devotion of this brave little woman, who endured seven hours of questioning on the stand, who told her relations with the deceased physician, and who has sat at her brother's side throughout the trial is believed to have been one of the contributing factors to Kendall's winning fight.

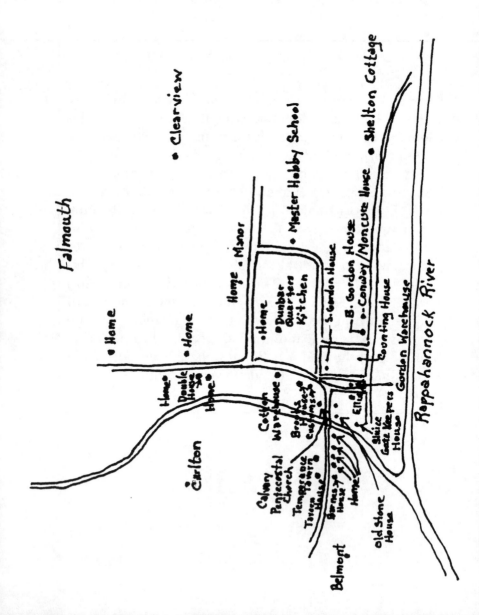

Whodunit?

WRIGHT (1893)

THE TOWN of Falmouth is located in Stafford County. Its location on the Rappahannock River testifies to its early settlement and its history as a port town as well as a milling center for the farmers in the area. During the nineteenth century, Falmouth shrank in size and importance. Today it is a charming town with an historic area of about three streets. The river continues to play a visible role in the character of the town.

Saturday, March 4, 1893, was inauguration day. A little sleet covered the ground. Bob Payne, who often visited Ida Wright at Mary Rennolds' house, was seen with Ida on Saturday on one of the boats that was moored on the Rappahannock River. On the same Saturday Lilly Wright had a baby.

Sunday, Ida stayed out all night, no one knows with whom she spent the night.

On Monday, March 6, Ida Wright, Sue Dawson and Cora Young were visiting on a boat on the Rappahannock River. From there Cora and Ida went to Emma Allen's. Then, Ida,

Cora and Emma Allen went to Messy Howard's "restaurant" to get something to eat. While there, they met Robert Jackson and Frank Taylor. Emma testified at the trial that only she and Ida went on to Messy Howard's. Ida had been drinking and was apparently in a good humor. While they were at Howard's eating place, Mary Rennolds came in, quite angry. Mary pulled a hat and cape from Ida and told her that she couldn't wear her daughter, Lilly's, hat. They quarreled. This developed into a scuffle in which the two women were fighting on the floor. Cora ran to get someone to help pull Mary off of Ida. Mary threatened to kill Ida if she came back to her house. She said she was tired of Ida's impudence and that she had to get her things out of her (Mary's) house immediately. Ida began to cry. Mary left and Ida sat for a while. Finally she said that she was going to Mary's and that either Mary would whip her or she would whip Mary.

Some witnesses believed that Ida was drunk. Robert Jackson and Frank Lucas or Taylor were in the dining room at this time. Messy (AKA Amensy Lewis) ordered the disorderly group to leave.

Robert Jackson, John Robinson and Andrew Kellam went to stand around King's. Ida came by, crying, saying that all she wanted was her clothes. According to the testimony of Robert Jackson, she went to Mary Rennolds' house and stood there a little while. Finally she went in. The men waited for a while and then left. Ida did not come out while they were there. Lilly, and Lizzie Hill, who was also present Mary Rennolds' house, stated that that evening, Mary and Ida got into a slapping match. According to Lilly Wright, later that night Ida went to church with Emma Allen. Maimie Jackson stated that after church, Ida went to Mary, Maimie's mother, and begged her pardon. Andrew Kellam stated that he was at church that night and did not see Ida there.

There is some confusion on the timing or date. However, what was established was that several witnesses, among them Mary Rennolds, Lilly Wright, Arie Rock and Lizzie Hill, saw a large quantity of fresh blood on the porch of the back door at

Mary Rennolds'. Lilly and Lizzie stated that the blood was there on March 6, Monday morning. Mary Rennolds and Arie Rock said the blood was on her porch Monday of the week following the fight.

Lilly Wright, the daughter of Mary Rennolds, had just had a baby and was at her mother's house. Ida was there too. Lilly and Lizzie Hill noticed the blood around the house and on Ida's clothing. When brought to Mary's attention, she asked Ida why she was bleeding. Ida said she couldn't help it. Lizzie thought it was Ida's menstruation. After questioning Ida about the blood, Mary went to work.

Tuesday, March 7, Ida went back to work cooking at Jacob Banks'. He asked her why she had not been at work on Sunday and Monday. Ida told him that she and her Aunt Mary [Rennolds] had a fight. According to Banks, she said that her Aunt Mary had been carrying a knife and Ida didn't know what to do about it. George Gaines, who was present at the time of this conversation, said he never heard Ida say anything to Jacob Banks about a knife.

On Wednesday, March 8, Ella Jones saw Ida outside of her house. At that time Ida was quite weak. She went in the house after seeing Ella and Ella never saw Ida again.

About a week after the fight, Amensy Lewis met Mary Rennolds on the street and Mary said she had given Ida a good beating last Monday and now Ida was sick and staying at her house.

Ida continued with her regular routine for a while, being seen about town. This was testified to by only Arie Rock. But by March 17, according to all accounts, Ida was in her bed, saying she didn't feel well.

Martha Grayson went to visit Ida at Mary's. She found her lying on an old pile of corn shucks, looking pitiful. She cried that she wanted some water, saying she hadn't had any all day. Martha brought her some and Ida drank "like she was famished."[1] Ida then asked for some "pot liqueur in salad." Martha, appalled at Ida's condition, told the people in the house that it was terrible that they let Ida suffer so. She then cooked some salad and carried it to Ida, who ate like she was starved. Martha asked Ida how long she had been sick and Lilly Wright said "several days." Lilly said that Ida had been cut. Martha asked to see the wound and Lilly said that Ida would not let anyone see it. Finally Ida was persuaded to show Martha her wound.

Martha stated, "I had never seen such a cut in my life."

Dr. A. C. Doggett, the coroner for Fredericksburg said that the wound was caused by a razor, knife or some other sharp instrument.[2] According to H. W. D. Martin (who later was called in to examine the body of Ida Wright) there was a sloughing wound extending about four inches from the lower part of the sacrum towards the anus. The sharp instrument apparently penetrated the rectum wounding the bowel, which caused blood poisoning.

The next day, Tuesday, Martha returned with Fanny Brown and the two women washed Ida, fixed up the corn shucks to make a bed, then put Ida to bed on it. On Wednesday the same two women came in and washed Ida again. While they were caring for her on Wednesday, Ida told them she hadn't done anything to anyone. Martha asked her who cut her. Ida looked around to see who was in the room and Mary Rennolds, who was in the room, said,

"Tell her what you told me."[3]

Every time Martha tried to get Ida to tell her who cut her, Lilly Wright would come up and say, "She ain't going to tell you."

One time Ida said in a low voice "Robert Jackson."

Then Lilly said, "She ain't going to tell you any more."

---

[1] Deposition of Martha Grayson at the Fredericksburg Corporation Court

[2] Deposition of A.C. Doggett, Coronor for Fredericksburg, VA

[3] Deposition of Martha Grayson

Martha tried on several occasions to get Ida to talk to her, but on each occasion, Lilly would keep talking in such a manner that Ida could not speak to Martha.

That Friday, Mary Rennolds and Annie Connor washed Ida. At first, when she was questioned, Ida would not say who cut her. Finally she said that Robert Jackson had cut her. Mary Rennolds stated that Ida and Fanny Childs had had some sort of disagreement about Robert Jackson "when the hobby horses were here." According to Emma Allen, Ida and Robert Jackson were quite good friends and had had no disagreement. Robert Jackson testified that he "had no fuss" with Ida.

Willis M. Robinson, Ida's minister, heard that Ida Wright had been cut badly and went to go see her at Mary Rennolds' on April 3. Martha Grayson, Martha Williams, Lilly Wright and Lilly's sister, Maimie Jackson, were with Ida. Ida was in bed when Willis got there. He asked her how she was. She replied that she felt badly. He told her he had heard that she was cut.

"Are you?" he asked.

"Yes, sir, I'm cut," she replied.

"Who cut you?"

"I can't tell," she said. "If I tell they say they will kill me and they say the officer will put me in jail."

Willis told her they would not kill her or put her in jail. "Tell me who cut you."

"Ambrose Taylor cut me," she said.

Then Lilly Wright shook her and said, "No, not Ambrose Taylor. He didn't cut you, it was Robert Jackson."

Then Ida said "I don't know who cut me. They cut me and they told me they amed [sic] kill me if I tell." Ida then got up on her elbows and knees and looked around anxiously to see who was in there. "I have been in jail a long time" she said "and don't want to be there again."[4]

---

[4] Testimony given by Rev. Willis Robinson in case styled *Commonwealth v. Reynolds*

OLD BUILDINGS IN FALMOUTH, VIRGINIA

B. Gordon House

Abandoned residence

Temperance Tavern

The impression that she made on Rev. Robinson by her anxiousness was that she referred to someone in the house as they and she seemed to be afraid to speak out what she knew because of this.

By April 6, Ida Wright was dead. At the time of the newspaper's report of the coroner's inquest on April 12, no arrests had been made, much to the indignation of the newspaper.[5]

Fredericksburg in 1796

FREDERICKSBURG, in the third quarter of the eighteenth century, was a thriving market town. While the tobacco trade was declining, merchant ships still plied the waters of the Rappahannock River, bringing goods from Europe and the West Indies as well as exporting goods produced in the Fredericksburg region and from other land-bound communities to the west. Several warehouses dotted the Rappahannock River on the Fredericksburg side, staffed by non-skilled labor.

Advertisements found in the *Virginia Herald,* a newspaper that covered the area of Fredericksburg and surrounding counties during the 1790's, reflect a way of living that, today, seems almost foreign in its simplicity and innocence.

---

[5] *Free Lance* newspaper, April 12, 1893, Fredericksburg, VA

Strayed from Lindsey's Mill near Port Royal some time last week, a bay stud horse about 14 hands high, 3 years old, two hind legs white, no brand. Whoever will deliver him to me shall receive three dollars reward.

William Drummond

Fredericksburg April 18, 1795

— ⁓⁓⁓ —

Those who have books in their possession, the property of the subscriber, are requested to return them immediately.

Mann Page

Mansfield Jan 28, 1795

There are some aspects of life that have not changed, again illustrated by articles from the *Virginia Herald.*

Good wages will be given to a person to attend a saw mill, who is well recommended as being acquainted with the business.

Jere. Morton

Spotsylvania 20 Apr 1795

— ⁓⁓⁓ —

To Be Rented
For the present year and possession given immediately.
Four tenements in Mr. Tayloe's brick buildings in this town.
For terms apply to

Thomas Hughes

Prices of goods available for sale in Fredericksburg were as follows:

Beef per barrel	$19.50
Pork per barrel	$25.00
Flour per barrel	$16.00
Candles per pound	.26
Butter per pound	.26
Leather per pound	.28
Brandy per gallon	$1 - 2.00
Soap per pound	.50

The theater in Fredericksburg was the site of plays and musical productions as well as a variation of the magic show. Seignior Falcon exhibited his "natural experiments," in 1795, that included a small "automaton" in a Turkish dress that would answer questions put to it, expulsion by electricity, the "penetrating Spy Glass" and the "Mysterious Candle."

Fredericksburg had periods of rapid and dramatic growth in its early years, followed by a slowed but rather steady growth period. (See population tables in the appendix). As Fredericksburg grew, the industry and the makeup of the work force within the city changed. While the early population had a large number of skilled artisans and merchants, the growing population contained an increasingly large number of laborers without any specialized skills. The increasing number of manufacturing concerns attracted this group of unskilled labor from surrounding counties, some of whom lived in the city. Others retained their residences outside of the town of Fredericksburg. A large percentage of these unskilled laborers were free blacks and mulattos.

Following the Revolution, large numbers of black slaves who performed military service for the American cause were freed. The sentiments of freedom also brought about large numbers of private manumissions from slave owners whose consciences were twinged by the articles within the Declaration of Independence and the Constitution. Still other slaves were able to buy their freedom and, sometimes, that of their families. These were usually skilled artisans who were able to command relatively significant wages or prices for their goods.

These policies of freedom were severely challenged in 1795 by a law that made private manumissions more difficult.

In addition to the cultural differences between the white population and the black population of Fredericskburg, there were major differences between blacks and whites in the eyes of the law.

Free blacks, whether considered mulattos or blacks, lived with severe restrictions on their associations and the professions they were allowed to follow. A law of 1792 prohibited free blacks from owning arms, meaning guns. They were not allowed to associate with slaves. They could not testify in court. Free blacks were also subject to curfew laws. Paradoxically, free blacks could own slaves.

Many free blacks worked as laborers, draymen, farm workers, blacksmiths, carpenters, barbers, seamstresses, washerwomen and midwives. Some free blacks served a period of indenture or apprenticeship as a means of learning a skill and/or earning a living. Those serving indentures usually served lengths of time similar to those served by white indentured servants. These indentures were generally documented in court records.

Blacks could generally shop in Fredericksburg, with some restrictions. However, most other facilities open to the public were segregated, such as ordinaries (or bars) and boarding rooms, churches and cemeteries.

This complex way of living created a great deal of tension among all groups. Combined with the transient nature of many of the unskilled workers, this provided a bubbling cauldron that repeatedly boiled over into crimes of violence.

STIRRS (1796)

IN THE Corporation of Fredericksburg on May 25, 1796, an inquisition was held at the house of Charity Winney on the body of one Gerrard Stirs, a free mulatto man from Fredericksburg. The coroner's inquest determined that on the night of May 24th, 1796, some person or persons unknown did kill and murder said Stir by inflicting on the calf of his left leg a wound. Some sharp instrument was determined to be the cause. The coroner's jury consisted of John Legg, Richard Peacock, William Herndon, William Pearson, Joseph Christy,

Site of John Benson's Tavern and possible site for the murder of
Gerrard Stirrs. Charity Winney may have rented rooms in the tavern.

Site of houses rented by free blacks in the eighteenth century.
Second possible site for the home of Charity Winney and possible site
of the murder of Gerrard Stirrs.

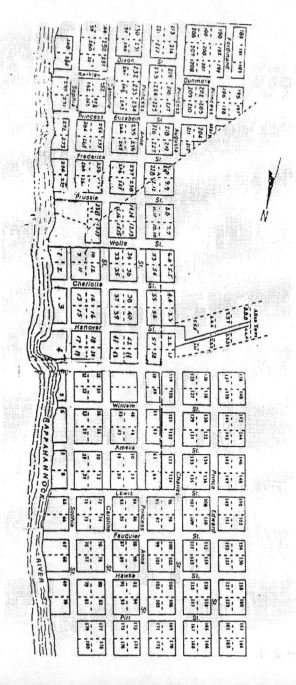

Charles Wardell, Henry White, William Smock, James Ross, John Welch, G. Hierskill and Jonathan Harris. [Author's note: all variations in spelling of the name Stirrs are replicated from the original documents.)

The map of Fredericksburg in 1796 (see map) shows the lot numbers for the city at that time. Most lot inhabitants can be accounted for by using the tax list for Fredericksburg for the same year. However, there is no lot owned by or inhabited by Charity Winney or any other person with the Winney last name. Since all renters and owners are listed on the tax list, except for mulattos and other poor free blacks, we can deduce that Charity Winney was either a free mulatto or a free black. Lots that were inhabited by free blacks were lots #7, 17, 45, 46, 236, 237, 209, 210, 211, 212, 202, 203, 77 & 227.

Lot #17 was John Benson's Tavern on Wolfe and Caroline Street. This tavern, right by the tobacco wharf, one of the warehouses that dotted the Fredericksburg shoreline of the Rappahannock River, seems to be the most likely site of the murder of Gerrard Stirrs.

However, another possible site of the murder was among the tenement houses on lots 211, 212 and 227.

The Stirrs surname was spelled several ways. While trying to determine who Gerrard Stirrs was, I explored the families of that name in Fredericksburg and the area surrounding it.

The Styers family in Fredericksburg, headed by Jacob Styers, owned a part of the Market Lot in 1797. In 1796, Jacob was renting a house from John Welch on Caroline Street, in an area that combined homes and businesses, much in the same way and location as today. The Styers Soap Boiling business was down two blocks and on the back street, or on the corner of Princess Anne Street and Fauquier Street. However, by 1802, Jacob Styers owned the #16 lot on Hanover Street, right across the street from Benson's Tavern. This lot was owned and occupied by Daniel Coyle in 1796. Whether this information, derived from tax records, proves that Gerrard Stirrs was a part of the Styers family has to be determined by further examination.

It seems highly possible that Gerrard Stirrs had been drinking heavily, previous to his murder. A cut in the leg could be easily cared for and not prove fatal to a person in possession of his wits. Additionally, blood takes longer to clot when there is alcohol in the blood. Since this leg wound was the only wound on his body, we have to assume that his death came about as a result of an unattended leg wound.

The murder weapon, a sharp instrument, is also a clue as to the identity of the murderer. Blacks and mulattos, free or enslaved, could not own arms of any kind. This would not, however, include a knife, ax or razor.

Based on descriptions of other mulatto Stirr/Sturrs from the area, we can guess that Gerrard was a dark mulatto, in his early twenties. He might have worked as a carpenter, cabinetmaker or in one of the warehouses along the Rappahannock. He probably had not been living in Fredericksburg very long. He may have moved from King George County.

George Jones, a son of Evan Jones of Stafford County, a descendant of one of Stafford County's original patent holders, was originally charged with the murder of Gerrard Stirrs. However, the case was never brought to court, charges apparently dropped due to lack of evidence or acknowledgment of having the wrong person.

Who killed Gerrard Stirrs?

KURZ (1934)

FEW actions create more indignation and fear than "getting away with murder." When an individual loses his life due to the actions (or sometimes inactions) of another, our sense of outrage against the perpetrator of the crime can often be manifested in the newspapers.

Such was the case that created the headlines in Fredericksburg on May 21, 1934:

TWO FOUND BADLEY BEATEN IN PARK.

The events surrounding and leading up to this murder began Wednesday, May 17, 1934. Gilbert Sullivan, son of Hunter Sullivan, was held up by a black man at 8 P.M. while he and a female companion were parked at a site near the Howison home. The man held an iron pipe and threatened the pair. He demanded that they give him all of their money. When Sullivan told them he didn't have any money the robber then demanded that they strip off all of their clothes. The young lady began to cry and plead for their freedom. Sullivan took out the $3.05 that he had in his pocket and told the robber that was all the money he had. The robber had them walk about 150 yards off the road and told them to stop. He said that he lived about 11,000 miles away from there so they better not try to find him. He then told them to get out of there. Sullivan and his companion ran from the man, got in their car and left. The last they saw of him, the robber was standing in the same spot they left him, watching them leave.

At the same place on Sunday night at about 9:15, a man with a similar description attempted to rob William H. Prasse and Evelyn Cooper, who were parked at the same spot. Prasse thought the man held a sawed-off shotgun. They were told to

put up their hands. They did so. Before any additional demands could be made by the robber, the headlights from an
oncoming car were seen, causing the would-be robber to re-
treat to some bushes. Prasse and Cooper immediately left the
area.

About an hour or less after the attack on Prasse and Cooper, some person beat Fannie J. Kurz and Milton Brown so severely that Miss Kurz died five days later while Brown remained in a semi-conscious state for over a week and was hos-
pitalized for nearly a month. They were found not 150 yards
from the road and about 75 yards from their car. The trees
and shrubs in the area where they were found had been
greatly trampled, leading police to believe that Brown had
struggled with his assailant in an attempt to prevent the robbery.

When Brown and Kurz were found, Brown's wallet containing $25.00 was missing and Kurz's clothes were disheveled,
indicating a search of her person for money or jewelry. Miss
Kurz was without shoes or stockings at the time she was found.
The robber did not take Brown's ring, however, which caused
investigators to theorize that rather than robbery, jealousy was
a motive for the attack. Family and friends of the victims dis-
counted the jealousy factor however. The couple had plans to
marry and neither had been known to have any relationships
that would cause a jealous attack. Miss Kurz did have a former
boyfriend who had threatened to get even with Brown for taking her away from him, but friends of the couple did not take
this as a serious threat.

When Brown regained consciousness, he said he remem-
bered nothing of the attack. Somewhat later, he said that he
recognized the person who attacked him as a black man who
had been to the garage where Brown worked several times.
Brown did not know his name.

About two months after Fannie Kurz died, "Blackie" Powell, a carnival worker who had been in the area when the at-
tacks occurred, was arrested and jailed while police investi-
gated him as a possible suspect. Powell spent his days in the

jail entertaining himself by making animal noises, from an ape to a lion. Police later released Powell. A friend of Powell's, also a carnival worker, known only by the name Woodson, was sought as another possible suspect. He was known to have lived in North Carolina but his whereabouts could not been determined.

Milton Brown and Fannie Kurz

Interestingly enough, after regaining consciousness, Milton Brown told investigators that on the night of the attack, he and Miss Kurz drove to the park where they had been in the habit of parking. Another car was parked there containing two men and a woman. One of the men was a man Brown recognized as the black man who had lately frequented the garage where Brown worked. The man had told Brown that he was from North Carolina. It appeared that the black man was fixing a tire on his car. Brown got out of the car and asked what the problem was. The man from North Carolina said he was having a problem with his tire. Brown bent over to look at the tire when he was struck on his head with a tire wrench.

When Brown raised himself in defense, the man struck him again. Brown doesn't remember anything after that point.

While this seems like a fairly vivid picture of a part of what happened, Dr. C. C. Coleman, the physician attending Brown, said that Brown's injuries were such that he probably would never recover his memory of the events of that night. He also advised investigators that little credence should be placed on the story given by Brown. Brown maintained his story, however.

Who killed Fannie Kurz?

Unusual Aspects

THE FOLLOWING is a transcription of a newspaper article in *The Virginia Star,* July 31, 1880.

TRACKED BY A WOMAN: AN ALLEGED MURDERER FROM BOWLING GREEN ARRESTED IN WASHINGTON CITY

A colored man named Henry Lee alias Jesse Dangerfield arrested at the insistence of a colored woman named Ella Johnson on suspicion of murdering Henry Williams, colored, at Bowling Green, Caroline County, VA is confined at police headquarters. So far all the information in the possession of the police is that derived from the woman, Johnson, who seems to have acted the part of detective with great success. The facts of the case, so far as can be learned are as follows. On the 16th instant Henry Williams, the uncle of Ella Johnson, went to the house of a man named Jim Wright, in Bowling Green. Lee, who had a grudge against Wright, also went to the house with one Walker Tolliver and calling Wright out,

assaulted him and was beating him when Williams inter-
fered.   Lee thereupon turned upon Williams and
plunged a long knife into his left side, killing him almost
instantly. Lee and Tolliver fled, but the latter was soon
captured. Lee, after skulking about the neighborhood
for several days and meeting with several adventures-in
one of which he was shot through the hand-made his
way to Stuart's landing, where he signaled the steamer
John W. Thompson and came to this city.

Ella Johnson, who lives at Hillsdale, went from there
to Bowling Green on a visit on the 17th instant and
when she arrived was shocked to learn of the murder of
her uncle. She returned to this city last Wednesday and
it so happened came on the same boat with Lee. She
happened to fall in with Lee, and though she did not
know him, had her suspicion, especially as he answered
well the descriptions of the fugitive.

She engaged him in a conversation and drew from
him the fact that he had a terrible fight with a man at
Bowling Green and in making his escape was shot
through the hand. The woman kept her own counsel,
and when they had arrived here showed Lee where a
friend of his in Uniontown named Beverly, whom he
wanted to see, resided and then informed the police.
Lee was arrested at Beverly's house by Sergeant
McCathran, and is now held at police headquarters. The
fact that he has a gunshot wound in the right hand col-
laborates the woman's story. Although he at first denied
the story altogether, he finally admitted that he had
struck a man at Bowling Green and was a fugitive on that
account. Lieutenant Eckloff has sent a letter to the sheriff of Caroline County acquainting him with the fact of
Lee's capture and Lee will be held subject to the sheriff's
order.

Washington Republican

THE JURORS of the Commonwealth of and for the body of the district composed of the counties of Spotsylvania, Caroline, King George, Stafford, Orange, Culpeper and Madison, do upon their oath present that Moses Burbridge, late of the parish of St. Thomas in the county of Orange aforesaid, laborer, not having the fear of God before his eyes, but being moved and seduced by the instigation of the Devil on the ninth day of October, in the year of our Lord one thousand eight hundred and one and in the twenty-sixth year of the Commonwealth, about the hour of eleven in the night of the same day, with force and arms...and upon one John Berry...feloniously, willfully and of his malice aforethought, did make an assault and that he, the said Moses Burbridge, with a certain knife of the value of six pence which the said Moses Burbridge then in his right hand ...[stabbed] the said John Berry in and upon the upper part of the belly above the navel and between the same and the breast bone of him...then immediately after striking and thrusting as aforesaid ...said Moses Burbridge with the same knife...immediately after the aforesaid striking and thrusting...[did strike and thrust] across the neck and windpipe of him the said John Berry.... The said John Berry...instantly died.

SO BEGAN the transcript from the court case of Moses Burbridge. While the murder of John Berry is an ugly depiction of unbridled angry passion, that is not what makes the case unusual.

Further in the lengthy court document we learn that Moses himself was not the one who held the knife that killed John

Berry. A Negro male slave by the name of Prince was the actual perpetrator of the crime. However, according to the court document, he was acting under the command, coercion and constraint of Moses Burbridge.

Indictments were issued for Jesse Hord, John Miller, Archibald Burden and William Steward in addition to that against Burbridge. Burbridge was the only one that went to trial. The slave, Prince, was never indicted.

Burbridge was found guilty of murder in the second degree and sent to the penitentiary for seven years on the 29th day of April 1802. There is nothing in any court record to indicate that Prince was in any way punished for his part in the crime.

Moses and Aaron Burbridge were the sons of William Burbridge, who died about 1756/57. The Burbridges were one of the early landowning families in Spotsylvania County. While their holdings were not extensive, they seemed to be respected by neighbors.

Moses was married to Fanny Haney on Christmas Eve 1798 in Spotsylvania.

There is not any record of John Berry in Spotsylvania County. The Berry family lived in Stafford County. Some members also lived in Fredericksburg. John may have been a member of the branch that lived in Fredericksburg.

 **Addenda**

CHRONOLOGY OF MURDERS

(Please note that the person listed as murderer may have only been accused and/or indicted, but not convicted. Suicides and manslaughter charges, except one, are not listed)

1689 - West (m)-an Indian (v)
1732 - Ambrose Madison (v)-Pompey (m)
1733 -
1734 -
1735
1736
1737 - Peter (m)-J. Riddle (v);
1738
1739
1740
1741
1742
1743
1744 - Tom (m)-Joe (v), Wick (v), Mungo (v), Rover (v);
1745 - Eve (m)-Peter Montague (v);
1746
1747
1748
1749

1750 - Alexander Crookshanks (m)- William Wheeler (v);

1751 - Cuffey (m)-Betty (v);

1752 - John Sparkes & John Trotman (m)-James Fox (v);

1753 - Edmund Waller (m)-Thomas Barnes (v);

1754

1755 - John Morton (m)-George James (v);

1756

1757

1758

1759

1760

1761 - Richard Johnston (m)-Richard Dunn (v); Daniel (m)-
        Pronton (v);

1762 - Peter (m)-Nicodemous (v), Jeffry (v); Cupid (m), Abel
        (m)-Frank (v);

1763 - Peter (m)-other slaves (v);

1765 - James Purvis (m)-Will (v);

1768 - Andrew Leitch (m)-Robert Haughes (v);

1771

1788 - J. Pettigrew (m)-Judith (v); Francis Purvis (v)- a slave
        (m);

1789

1790 - Ritchie (v)-Glassell (m);

1791

1792 - John Brock Jr. (v)-Tom & Joe, slaves (m); Nancy Clark
        (v)-David Yowell (m); Thomas Ross (m)-James Williams
        (v); Abraham Van Horne (v);

1793 - William Crane (v)-George T. Tod (m); T. Graves (v)-F.
        Fant (m); G. Bush (v)-M. Bush (m);

1794 - Benjamin Grymes (m)- Robert Galloway (v);

1795 - John Morton (v); Daniel Branham Jr. (v)-James Blake
        (m);

1796 - William Fox (m)-Rippon (v); Gerrard Stirs (v)- un-
        known murderer;

1797 - John Key Kendall (v)-Josephus Ambler (m); John
        Hilldrup (m)-Benjamin Bryant (v);

1798 - J. Keegan (m)-S. Keegan (v);

1799 - James Brazel ( ); Major (m);
1800 - Vincent Branson (m)-Lydia Branson (v);
1801 - George Hughlette (v)-John Carter; John Berry (v)-
      Prince a slave of Moses Burbridge (m);
1802 - Underwood ( ); Ramsey infant (v) Betty Ram-
      sey/Ransdale (m); J. Witherall (v)-E. Jenkins (m);
      Squire (v)-John Cason (m);
1803 - Lucy Stevens (m)-baby girl Stevens (v); Thomas Ryan
      (v)-Samuel Jones (m); Thornton (m)&(v)-Conway
      (m)&(v);
1804 - Jonathan Garrott (v)-Alexander Burke (m); 1 negro (v);
      B. Russell ( );
1805 - Edmund Gatewood (m)-Burton Hopkins (v); James
      Waug (v)-Allan Jones (m); W. Stratton (m)-B. Stratton
      (v); George Jones (m)- Elizabeth Green (v);
1806 - J. Giles (v)-Alex. MaGee (m); G. Garland (v);
1807 - Judy a slave (v)-Garner (m)
1808 - Peter Daniel (v); Sam Hill (m)- G. Sommerson (v); John
      Seddon (v); Wm. Kirk (m)- Harry (v);
1809 - John Skinker ( ), William Skinker( )
1810
1811
1812 - John Delevus (v)-Jacob Young (m);
1813 - Betsy Whitacre (v);
1814 - Cromwell (v)-Thomas McKenny (m);
1815 - M. G. Burke (m);
1816 - George a slave (v); infant Jane Doe (v); John Goss (v)-
      John King (m);
1817 - Jesse Simpson (v);
1818
1819
1820
1821
1822
1823 - Robin a slave (v)-Thomas Alsop (m);
1824 - Henry Ferguson (v)-Eliza Newton (m);
1825

1826

1827 - Charles Payne (v)-William Johnston (m); infant John
　　　　Doe (v);

1828 - Pierce Walker (m);

1829 - Armistead (v)-Thomas Chew (m);

1830 - Ben (v)-Henry Johnson (m);

1831

1832

1833

1834 - John Shepherd (v)-Emanuel Martin (m);

1835 - Eliza Grymes (m)-George Grymes (v);

1836 - John Shepherd (v)-Emanuel Martin (m);

1837 - infant Jane Doe (v);

1838

1839 - William Richardson (v)-Betsy Richardson (m);

1840 - George Jett (v)-Wm. Rose (m); infant Jane Doe (v);

1841

1842 - infant John Doe (v);

1843 - Catherine Weedon (v)-M. Weedon (m); Staples Thomp-
　　　　son (v)-Jefferson Richmond (m); G. Ware (m)-W.
　　　　Lewis (v);

1844 - James Cavenough (v)-William Darby/Dailey Sullivan
　　　　(m);

1845 - W. Jennings (v)-Mills (m); Gerard Puzey (v)-
　　　　Malvina/Mildred Puzey(m);

1846

1847 - Thomas Minor (v)-Linsey Owens (m); Thomas Handley
　　　　(v)-G. Jeffries (m); Tom (v)- L.Owens (m); infant John
　　　　Doe (v);

1848

1849 - A. Anderson (v)

1850 - William Hewett (v)-Jeremiah Carter (m); Brown (m)-
　　　　___gett (v); Edwards (v);

1851 - Emanuel Byram (v)-Wm. H. Worthington (m); R. Talley
　　　　(v);

1852

1853 - Frederick B. Brown (v); Wm. L. Warring (v)- Jesse or
        Isaac Fisher (m);
1854 - Joseph Ashton (v); infant John Doe (v);
1855 - infant John Doe (v);
1856 - infant Jane Doe (v);
1857 - Houston (v)-James Crowley (m); Mr. Anderson (v); Mrs.
        Cliff (v)-Reuben (m)
1858 - Griffin (v); Henry Bowyer (m); Mr. Carver (v);
1859 - James Heslip (v)-Eliza Heslip (m); infant John Doe (v);
1860
1861 - infant Jane Doe (v);
1862 - Michael Russell (v)-Thomas Ryan/Roys (m); Henry I.
        Thomas (v)-Rufus Farrer (m); Jerred Beach (v);
1863 - W.A. Jones (m)-his child (v);
1864 - R.W. Bowling (m)-James Harrow (v);
1865 - H.B. Lewis (m)-Dr. Rose (v);
1866
1867
1868 - infant Doe (v);
1869 - Samuel Folke (v)& John McKeaters/McNealus (v)-
        James Bullock (m);
1870 - Mr. Jett;
1871 - T. Toombs (v)-A.J. Norton (m); Alice Vaughn (v)-
        Richard Hudson (m);
1872 - Elizabeth Lucas (v)-Sylvia Lucas (m);
1873
1874
1875 - Sophia Roy (v)-William Henry Robinson (m);
1876
1877 - Tayler Flinch (m)-Paul Newton (v); Jesse Wright (v)-
        Charles E. Pendleton (m);
1878
1879 - Withers (v)-Clara Withers (m);
1880 - H. Williams (v)-Henry Lee (m); Amie Spence/Moore
        (m)-Oscar Spence (v); McCracken (v);
1881 - Elliot Brown (m);
1882 - infant Jane Doe (v);

1883 - Shlritz (m);
1884
1885
1886
1887- Lawson Bledsoe (v)
1888 - D. Pryor (v)-T. Edwards/Jackson (m);
1889 - H. Johnston (v)-Jordan Washington, R. Washington, G.
    Lewis (m);
1890
1891 - M. McCracken (v)-T. McCracken (m);
1892 - C. Washington (v)-M. A. Gately Sr. (m);
1893 - Ida Wright (v)-Mary Rennolds (m)?;
1894 - H. N. Harrison (v)-C. Brummett (m);
1895
1896
1897
1898 - Lewis Bailey (m);
1899
1900 - Wm. Gunn (v)-A. Jackson (m); Anne E. Hawkins (v) -
    B.F. Hawkins (m); Daniel E. Lee (v) -
1901 - Lucy McCandlish (v); Ida Perry (v); James Wharton (v);
1902 - James Cooper (v); Nancy Stanley (v);
1903
1904
1905
1906
1907 - Lucy Page (v)-Henry Deane Jr. (m);
1908 - John Doe (v);
1909
1910
1911
1912 - M. & M. Thornton (v)-F. Hargrove (m);
1913
1914
1915
1916
1917

1918
1919
1920
1921
1922
1923
1924 - Jesse Foster (m)-John Johnson (v); Robert Powell (v)-
        Charles Kendall (m); T. Howard (v)-John Stevens (m);
        Thornton Grayson (m)-Caesar Noel (v);
1925 - C. Shelton (m)-C. Baker (v);
1926
1927
1928
1929
1930
1931
1932
1933
1934 - Fannie Kurz (v); Bessie Reamy (m)-Robert H. Barrow
        (v); Mr.& Mrs. Coleman (v);
1935
1936 - Carter (v)-Bolling (m);
1940 - M. Prince (m);
1950 - R. J. Spence (m)(had 2 victims); J. Buckner (m);
1964 - J. Bumbrey (m);
1970
1971
1972
1973
1974
1975
1976
1977
1978 - Stafford had 1, + Gavis (v)
1979 - Stafford had 1
1980 - Stafford had 4
1981 - 9

1982 - 2
1983 - 5
1984 - 5
1985 - 9
1986 - 8
1987 - 8
1988 - 4
1989 - 7
1990 - 5
1991 - 6
1992 - 11
1993 - Stafford had 2, Caroline & King George had 0
1994 - Stafford had 1, Caroline had 2, King George had 4

Totals, when listed by a single number are the total number for all jurisdictions. Where only partial information was available, totals for those jurisdictions were shown individually.

POPULATION SCHEDULES

Spotsylvania

1734	1,035	(tithables only) (2)	
1740	1,395	"	(7)
1768	2,307	"	(2)
1769	2,307	"	"
1770	2,250	"	"
1772	2,517	"	"
1773	2,760	"	"
1774	2,800	"	"
1775	2,933	"	(7)
1776	2,933	"	(2)
1777	2,703	"	"
1778	2,752	"	"
1780	3,252	"	(7)
1781	3,238	"	"
1782	3,238	"	"
1783	11,252	population	
1790	11,253	"	(3)
1810	10,687	"	(3)
1843	4,024	tithables (2)	
1844	4,100	"	(2)
1845	4,067	"	(2)
1846	4,056	"	(2)
1847	3,979	"	(2)
1848	3,966	"	(2)
1849	4,129	"	(2)
1850	10,853	"	(3)

Culpeper

1790	22,105 (3)
1840	11,393 (3)
1900	14,123 (3)

Caroline

1787	5,669 Tithables (10)
1788	5,642 Tithables (10)
1789	5,607 Tithables (10)
1790	5,727 Tithables (10)
1790	17,489 population (3)
1791	5,681 Tithables (10)

Fredericksburg

1732	6 (figure given by Col.Byrd)
1740	375	(1)
1750	600	(1)
1760	661	(1)
1769	These figures are incorporated in Spotsylvania's figure
1770	780	(1)
1780	1,000	(6)

Figures up to this date are included in Spotsylvania's population figures. After 1782 the figures reflect Fredericksburg as a town only.

1782	1,020	(1)
1787	521 (this is only male tithables over 21)
1790	1,485 (whites only) (3)
1810	2,509	(3)
1820	3,076	"
1830	3,307	"
1835	3,308	(5)
1840	3,974	(3)
1850	4,062	"
1860	4,970	"

Stafford

1724	624 families (9)
1785	2,483 (whites only) (3)
1790	9,588	(3)
1810	9,830	(3)
1830	500 (Falmouth only) (5)
1850	8,093	(3)

King George

| 1776 | 400 military men only (8) |
| 1790 | 7,366 | (3) |

LIST OF ACTING JUSTICES AND SHERIFFS

SPOTSYLVANIA COUNTY

Date Qualified	Names of Justices and When Sheriff
7 Aug 1722	William Bledsoe
2 Jun 1724	Thomas Chew
5 Apr 1725	Thomas Chew
7 Jun 1726	Goodrich Lightfoot
2 May 1727	Goodrich Lightfoot
4 Jun 1728	Larkin Chew
1 Apr 1729	Edwin Hickman
2 Jul 1730	Edwin Hickman
6 Jul 1731	William Johnson
1 May 1733	Joseph Brock
6 May 1735	Joseph Thomas
5 Jul 1737	John Chew
3 Jul 1739	Larkin Chew
4 Aug 1741	John Taliaferro
2 Aug 1743	John Minor
3 Jul 1744	William Robinson
5 Aug 1746	John Waller
6 Sep 1748	Richard Tutt
4 Sep 1750	John Thornton
3 Sep 1751	John Thornton
4 Aug 1752	John Chew
6 Aug 1754	Larkin Chew
3 Aug 1756	Rice Curtis
1 Aug 1758	William Carr
1 Sep 1758	Robert Jackson
6 Sep 1762	Charles Dick
3 Dec 1764	Beverley Winslow
18 Oct 1766	Joseph Brock
7 Nov 1768	John Carter
15 Nov 1770	Robert Goodloe
20 Nov 1772	John Crane
17 Nov 1774	William Smith
19 Dec 1776	Charles Yates
19 Nov 1778	Edward Herndon

7 Jan 1794	Thomas Minor Sheriff Nov 1812
2 Jul 1799	Samuel Sale Sheriff Nov 1816
4 Nov 1800	Benjamin Waller Sheriff Nov 1818
6 Sep 1803	Hugh T.W.Mercer Sheriff Nov 1820
	(resigned)
4 Apr 1805	Waller Holladay
7 Jan 1806	George Hamilton Sheriff Nov 1822
7 Jan 1806	William Waller Sheriff Nov 1824
6 Nov 1809	John Lipscomb (dead)
5 Nov 1810	Joseph Herndon (resigned)
2 Jul 1810	Brodie S. Hull (dead)
6 Aug 1810	Robert Crutchfield
1 Nov 1813	John McCoull
1 Nov 1813	Malcolm Hart
1 Nov 1813	Therit Towles
1 Nov 1813	Gabriel Long
4 Aug 1817	Richmond Lewis
3 Aug 1818	William G. Sears (dead)
4 Jan 1819	John S. Wellford
6 Nov 1820	Dabney Herndon (dead)
2 Oct 1820	William H. Fulcher
5 Aug 1822	Archibald Hart
2 Dec 1822	Benjamin Coleman
5 Aug 1822	Thomas Poindexter Jr. (removed)
5 Aug 1822	Philip Thornton (resigned)
6 Dec 1824	Sanford Chancellor
1825	Oscar M. Crutchfield
5 Sep 1825	Benjamin Rawlings
1825	John C. Brown
5 Sep 1825	William White
5 Sep 1825	Eaton Stanard
5 Sep 1825	Claiborne Wiglesworth (dead)
5 Sep 1825	Thomas C. Waller
1827	John M. Anderson
1827	Thomas Chandler
1827	Reuben T. Thom
1827	Hugh M. Patton
1827	Sim B. Goodloe
1827	William Beazley
1828	Edmund P. White
1828	James D. Dillard

1828	George Turner
1829	Lewis S. Halladay
1829	Oscar M. Crutchfield
1831	Robert Churchfield
1831	Therit Towles
1831	Gabriel Long
1831	Edward Hull
1833	Hubbard T. Minor
1833	William Crump
1833	Claiborne Duvall
1833	James Hart
1833	Joseph Alsop
1837	Lewis A. Boggs
1837	Absalom Row
1837	Lewis Johnson
1837	John C. Stanard
1837	Melzi S. Chancellor
1841	John H. Wallace
1841	William C. Rathrock
1841	Marshal Johnson
1841	John I. Berry
1841	John M. Waller
1846	John C. Jerrell
1846	William P. Bowen
1846	Franklin Slaughter
1846	Warren A. Wigglesworth
1846	Montgomery Slaughter
1846	George P. Goodloe

LIST OF SHERIFFS IN KING GEORGE COUNTY

1776	John Taliaferro Jr.
1777	Townsend Dade
1781	Francis Conway
	Thomas Jett

CAROLINE COUNTY SHERIFFS

1729	William Woodford
1731	John Taliaferro
1732	Robert Fleming
1734	Walter Chiles
1735	Robert Farish
1737	George Goodloe
1738	Head Lynch
1740	William Taliaferro
1741	Lawrence Battaile
1742	John Micou
1743	John Taylor
1744	George Hoomes
1745	Robert Taliaferro
1747	Thomas Buckner
1750	James Taylor
1751	George Hoomes
1753	Richard Buckner
1755	Thomas Johnston
1757	Edward Dixon
1758	Phillip Taylor
1759	Robert Gilchrist
1760	John Sutton
1762	Francis Taylor Jr.
1763	John Sutton
1764	Anthony Thornton
1765	William Goode
1767	William Tyler
1769	James Taylor Jr.
1773	Walker Taliaferro
1775	John Buckner
1778	Thomas Lowry
1780	John Armistead

MISCELLANEOUS WEATHER NOTES

OCCASIONALLY weather conditions may play a part in a murder or in how a case is solved. The following are some notes on the weather that were taken from the local newspapers.

A blizzard hit Fredericksburg on March 1, 1755. Drifts were piled so high that work on building roads had to cease. In a letter to William Braddock, Sir John St. Clair states that "I have this for it, that the weather changes in this Climate every twenty four hours." [Some things never change.]

There was intense heat during the summer of 1850 and record setting heat in 1934.

A severe snowstorm began on Saturday January 17, 1857. Ice blocks 11" thick were taken from the Rappahannock River about this time.

On Sunday March 1, 1857 and on Monday March 2, 1857, there were extremely high winds that nearly swept the water from the Rappahannock River, Aquia Creek and the Potomac River.

On Sunday, April 29, 1877, about four o'clock "a most destructive hailstorm visited that portion of Stafford...lying from Falmouth to Marlboro Point in a line from one to four miles in width. ... A dark and angry looking cloud extended from the South all around the Western and Northern horizons. As the cloud rose it underwent wonderful and beautiful changes of color from black to bright green and purple and presented one of the most remarkable spectacles ever witnessed in [Stafford]."

Hail was purported to be up to four feet deep in areas where it had drifted. It was four inches deep when measured at a level point near Potomac Run. The destructive hailstorm damaged roofs, tore shutters from windows and broke glass everywhere along the path. Fruit and forest trees were stripped of foliage. Growing wheat was beaten to the ground. In one instance, a man and his horse were caught outdoors during the storm. The man was battered and the horse disabled.

Once the storm passed, a gentle breeze wafted across town.

June 10, 1924, in Woodford, Caroline County, it was reported that the farmers in that vicinity took advantage of the short dry spell to plant corn. There had been severe storms the previous Sunday afternoon and Monday. From comments about the harvest and livestock, it seems that there had been a prolonged period of rain, with little time in between storms for the land to dry out.

The *Free Lance* reported on 1 November 1900 that the last four months were the hottest recorded ever.

Index